EL TOQUE FINAL

postres, pan, salsas, sopas, cremas, chutneys y más de el piano

el piano's desserts, breads, sauces, soups, chutneys and more

THE FINAL TOUCH

Magdalena Chávez

www.el-piano.com

texto y recetas - text & recipes
2012 © Magdalena Chávez
fotos - photographs
2012 © Florence Millett Sikking, Elena Jackson,
Anne Sikking
editora - editor
Florence Millett Sikking
colaboradoras de recetas - recipe collaboration
Shonét Hockley
Elena Jackson
Thushanthi Liyanage
Miriam Perea
Mayra Marín Salazar
Florence Millett Sikking
&
Elaina Smith
consulta de idiomas - language consultancy
María Inmaculada Marchena Márquez
Liz Chadwick
Leah Amber Jackson-Blake

first published 2012 by
SQUAW PIES
an imprint of

COLLAGE INTERNATIONAL LTD
www.collage-international.com

™ registered trademark of Collage International Ltd

introducción foreword

Cuando se lanzó la serie MANO hace 10 años, el primer libro, MANO a BOCA, fue el primer libro de recetas de El Piano. Desde entonces otros cocineros han contribuido a la serie hasta 2009 cuando que se publicó MANO a MANO los platos salados de el piano, *que se ha vendido por todo el mundo.*

Durante muchos años nuestros clientes nos han pedido las recetas de los postres de El Piano. A veces se las mandamos por email o las publicamos en la página web o, incluso, respondiendo a clientes en los restaurantes en el momento, se las apuntamos en un trozo de papel...

Por fin, con EL TOQUE FINAL, *nuestras recetas de postres y dulces, además de algunos de nuestros platos salados nuevos, se encuentran en un libro a disposición de todos. También hemos incluido recetas para hacer pan y tofu e información general sobre cómo funcionan las recetas. Muchas de las salsas, chutneys y condimentos que se asocian con El Piano están incluidos. Son estos sabores especiales que le dan a la comida ese algo extra...el toque final.*

Nuestra atención a la comida vegana y sin gluten está basada en muchos factores, entre ellos el placer de crear una comida para todos.

When the HAND series was launched ten years ago, El Piano's *HAND to MOUTH* was the first book. Since then others have added to the series, and then, in 2009, *HANDING it ON el piano's book of savouries*, was published and has sold widely.

People have asked us over the years for our dessert recipes. Sometimes we send these recipes by email, publish them on the website, or even, at times, in response to requests from diners, have jotted them on the back of an envelope.

At last, in *THE FINAL TOUCH*, our dessert recipes, along with a few of our latest savouries, are in book form. We also include bread and tofu making, as well as generic information about how recipes work. Many of the sauces, chutneys and condiments that people associate with El Piano are included. These often give a meal that special extra something...the final touch.

Our focus on vegan and gluten-free food is based on many factors, among them the pleasure of being able to provide food for all.

Magdalena Chávez
fundadora/founder
Granada 2012

3

agradecimientos

Es imposible que una persona escriba recetas sola. Hacen falta proveedores y personas que prueben y verifiquen que las recetas sean correctas.

Verduras locales como las de Yorkshire Chillies y La Huerta Santa María, ingredientes básicos y exóticos de Biogran, Tortillas Nagual, Suma, La Finestra sul Cielo y Country Products y las cerámicas de Artesanía Álvarez, han contribuido todos a este libro.

Y l@s cociner@s...¿Como se podría haber hecho esto sin Florence y Mayra, Elaina y Thushi, sin Elena, Mike Brid, Miriam y Shonét? Años de innovar Y llevar a cabo las tareas diarias. Gracias a todos.

No habría un libro sin (io con menos!) fallos sin Liz, Inma y Leah...

Gracias a Julia y Melanie por aclarar algunos temas de otros libros nuestros. Vuestro apoyo ha ayudado a que este libro esté mejor escrito.

Alguien tiene que vender la comida y los libros, lo hacemos todos, pero nadie con tanto estilo como Bob y César. Y alguien tiene que cuidar las cuentas. Gracias Bill.

Y, por supuesto, por último, está USTED. Nos ha apreciado y ha contribuido a pagar nuestros sueldos. Espero que usted se sienta orgulloso de nuestros logros, que de alguna manera, son también suyos.

acknowledgements

Recipes are impossible to write alone. Someone has to provide the ingredients, or eat the results, notwithstanding test them.

Veg from local suppliers like Yorkshire Chillies, La Huerta Santa María, dried goods & exotica through Biogran, Tortillas Nagual, Suma, La Finestra sul Cielo & Country Products, beautiful ceramics from Artesanía Álvarez, have all made this book.

Then of course the cooks. How could this have been done without Florence & Mayra, Elaina & Thushi, without Elena, Mike Brid, Miriam & Shonét? Years of inventiveness AND daily grind with an open heart. Thank you all.

Nor could we have done without Liz, Inma & Leah...Without them there would MORE errors...

Thanks also to Julia & Melanie who took time to write to us for clarification on our other books & whose efforts have hopefully made this one better.

Someone has to sell the food & books, which we all do, but few with such flair as Bob & César. Marjorie sorts the paperwork & someone has to care for the cash. Thanks Bill.

Finally of course there has been YOU. You have praised us & paid our wages. I hope you are proud of our achievements. In many ways they are yours.

acerca de este libro   about this book

La mayoría de las recetas son fáciles pero este libro NO es para principiantes.

Lo que hemos hecho es reunir años de trabajo y técnicas, que usamos a diario en las cocinas internacionales de EL PIANO, que si se adoptan resultan en platos rápidos y nutritivos.

Como cualquier habilidad, la perfección viene de practicar. El objetivo principal de este libro es aumentar la confianza de tal manera que se pueda deshacer del libro...

Con el conocimiento de cómo funcionan los ingredientes, por ejemplo levaduras, harinas, edulcorantes, l@s cociner@s tienen la oportunidad de desarrollar sus propias recetas.

Esperamos que si apunta lo que le gusta a usted, a los amigos y a la familia, pueda ampliar su propia colección de recetas. Liberación de las recetas, en vez de seguirlas detalladamente, resulta en comidas de las propias manos de l@s cociner@s que se pueden compartir y transmitir a los demás, como hemos hecho aquí.

While the recipes are mostly easy, and beginners should be able to tackle them, this is a book for the creative chef rather than for an out and out beginner.

What we have done is bring together a body of work and techniques that are used daily in the EL PIANO kitchens worldwide and which, if adopted, should bring quick wholesome results.

As with any skill, practice can result in perfection. However, the objective of this book is to build confidence so that the recipe book can eventually be ditched...

With a knowledge of how things work, such as raising agents, flours and sweetners, the opportunity exists for any cook to develop their own personal recipes.

Noting down what appeals to you, to your friends and family, and then compiling your own collection of favourites is our hoped for outcome. Freedom from recipes, rather than slavishly following them, results in something from a cook's own hand which may be shared and passed on, as we have done here.

contents

índice

contents índice

el almacén - the storeroom
EL PIANO GRANADA

braham Lincoln dijo, 'no puedes complacer a todo el mundo, todo el tiempo'. Las salsas son la solución para la variación de gusto (y la manera de desmentir al Honesto Abe).

Son también el antídoto a la enfermedad mental cuando cada persona quiere un sazón diferente... De niña en una familia grande, mi padre, respondiendo a muchas demandas diferentes, nos gritó desde la cocina 'ya no trabajo en la comida rápida'. Se refería a los años que trabajó con los hermanos McDonalds en San Bernardino, California, donde existía la posibilidad de pedir muchas variaciones. (Negó su oferta de ser socio diciendo que 'nadie podrá ganar dinero fabricando hamburguesas'...).

Las salsas duran para muchas comidas, son vistosas y sirven también para conservar las verduras de una cosecha grande.

Sobre todo, son increíblemente fáciles de hacer.

As Abraham Lincoln famously said, 'you cannot please all of the people, all of the time.' Sauces are the solution to the varied palate (and disprove Honest Abe).

They are also the cook's safeguard of sanity. My father, in response to different preferences, was fond of shouting from the kitchen, 'I'm not a short-order cook anymore' referring to the years he had worked with the McDonalds brothers in California. (He declined to become a partner saying, 'there will never be any money in hamburgers'...).

Sauces will last for many meals, look wonderful and often have the added benefit of conserving garden gluts. Furthermore, they are fabulously easy to make.

sweet sauces   salsas dulces

Sweet sauces are extremely versatile as pie fillers, as glazes for cakes and also provide the basis for puddings.

Hot sauces like custard are not just a topping for pies and crumbles but served alone are also an excellent way to nourish people, young and old alike, who might otherwise fail to take in the minimum recommended daily nutritional requirements.

BIRD'S CUSTARD, which is the well-known British brand of custard, was developed by Alfred Bird for his ailing wife. Essentially it is a thick flavoured milk and our versions are not much different - thick flavoured and sweetened water, soya milk, rice milk or fruit juice.

Because we use a variety of flours in our sauces there is the option to chop and change. This not only means freedom to make a sauce even when one flour is missing from the kitchen, it also means that people with eating restrictions can enjoy sauces again and by using many different flours we can introduce variety into the diet and thereby ensure a more balanced result.

Las salsas dulces son muy versátiles como relleno de tartas, coberturas para pasteles y como base para todo tipo de postre.

Salsas dulces y calientes como la crema inglesa, CUSTARD, se pueden usar para acompañar tartas, y también se pueden servir solas. Así, nos dan una oportunidad excelente para alimentarnos, sobre todo a los jóvenes y a las personas mayorès. Las salsas dulces pueden ser una forma fácil de tomar muchos ingredientes nutritivos.

En nuestras salsas usamos una gran variedad de harinas, y siempre existe la opción de sustituir una por otra. Esto significa que siempre se puede elaborar salsas aunque falte algún ingrediente. También quiere decir que él que no pueda tomar algunos ingredientes por razones de alergias puede volver a disfrutar de las salsas. El uso de tantas harinas diferentes asegura mayor equilibrio en la dieta.

classic bechamel sauce is fundamental to sauce making, whether sweet or savoury - it is the basis of hollandaise sauce, of cheese sauce, of carbonara, of mushroom sauce and so the list goes on...
the steps are simple yet essential for success and need to be followed regardless of which fat or which flour is used...

heat the fat, if margarine, heat it until melted, if oil, it should not be smoking
REMOVE from the heat and stir in the flour
ONLY when the flour is FULLY COATED return to the heat briefly
REMOVE from the heat and stir in the liquid little by little, at each stage ensuring that all lumps are dissolved
ONLY WHEN ALL THE LIQUID IS ADDED and there are NO LUMPS return to the heat
STIR constantly until the sauce thickens
use the stick blender for quick 'repairs'

Para cada litro de líquido (combinaciones de leche, agua, vino, zumo) usar 3 CDA de grasa y 3 CDA de harina. Sal y pimienta al gusto.

For every litre of liquid (combinations of milk, water, wine, juice) use 3 TBL of fat and 3 TBL of flour. Salt and pepper to taste.

la salsa bechamel es una salsa clásica y su proceso de elaboración es fundamental para hacer salsas dulces tanto como salsas saladas - es la base de la salsa holandesa, salsa con queso, salsa carbonara...
los pasos son sencillos pero imprescindibles para buen resultado - es necesario seguirlos da igual la grasa y harina que elija usar

calentar la grasa - si es margarina hasta que se derrita - si es aceite no debe echar humo
QUITAR DEL FUEGO y añadir la harina
cuando la harina esté completamente CUBIERTA de grasa reponer a cocinar brevemente
QUITAR DEL FUEGO y añadir el líquido poco a poco asegurando con cada gota que los GRUMOS estén disueltos
reponer a cocinar y remover constantemente hasta que la salsa espese
usar la batidora para repararla si hace falta

chocolate & vanilla custards
cremas de chocolate y vainilla

By using water instead of soya or rice milk, the custard is lighter and easier to pour.

For chocolate custard use 1 TBL rice flour to 1L water. Add 1 TBL cocoa plus pure vanilla, sugar and salt to taste. Bring to the boil slowly.

Chilli powder is optional.

Si usamos agua en vez de leche de arroz o soja, la crema es más ligera y más fácil de verter.

Para la crema de chocolate usar 1 CDA de harina de arroz por cada 1L de agua. Añadir 1 CDA de cacao y vainilla pura, azúcar y sal al gusto. Cocinar lentamente hasta que hierva.

Una pizca de cayena es opcional.

For vanilla custard use 1 TBL rice flour to 1L liquid. This can be water, milk or fruit juice of whatever type. Add pure vanilla, sugar and salt to taste. Bring to the boil slowly. A pinch of turmeric (haldi) gives a tint of yellow. The colour intensifies with time, so go easy.

Para la crema de vainilla usar 1 CDA de harina de arroz por cada 1L de líquido. El líquido puede ser agua, leche o zumo de cualquier tipo. Añadir vainilla pura, azúcar y sal al gusto. Cocinar lentamente hasta que hierva. Una pizca de cúrcuma es opcional y da un toque de amarillo a la crema. El color se pone más intenso con el tiempo. Añadirla con cuidado.

toppings can add flavour and sweetness

they can also act as protection against drying out and enhance presentation by adding brilliance and shine

whatever your preferences there are many toppings, including mashed up fruit with or without sugar

las coberturas dan sabor y endulzan

también pueden proteger contra la sequedad y mejorar la presentación con un toque de brillo

cualquiera sea el motivo, hay muchas opciones de coberturas incluyendo fruta fresca batida, con o sin azúcar

cake topped with fruit juice only

pastel con solo zumo de fruta por encima

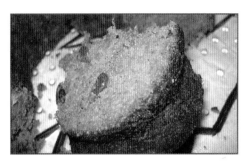

250g of margarine beaten with 250g of icing sugar

250g de margarina batida con 500g de azúcar glacé

water and sugar drizzled over the top with fresh fruit to decorate

agua y azúcar encima adornado con fruta fresca

500g icing sugar beaten with the juice of ½ lemon

500g de azúcar glacé mezclado con el zumo de ½ limón

accompaniments   para acompañar

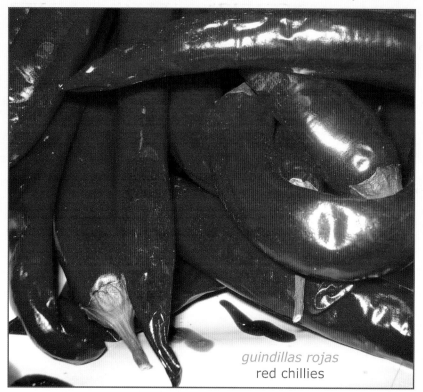

guindillas rojas
red chillies

The word chutney is Hindi and means 'good to eat'. This initially Indian tradition of savoury accompaniments, pickles, chuntneys and relishes, found its way into British cuisine during the British Raj and from there entered the food traditions of the world.

From the simplest of sauces like raitha, to moisten dry curries and fritters, to the most complex flavours of mango chutney with upwards of 30 ingredients, the purpose is to enhance the flavour of the main dish. Some take days to prepare, some can be created in seconds...Our customers at EL PIANO have loved us for them over many years and some say they come just for the chutneys!

Chutney es una palabra hindi y significa 'bueno para comer'.

La tradición de condimentos como chutney, pickle y relish viene originalmente de la India y entró en la cocina británica por el Raj Británico de la India, y, desde allí entró en la cocina del mundo.

Desde las salsas más sencillas como raitha, para acompañar los currys secos y las frituras, hasta las salsas más complejas como el chutney de mango con más de 30 ingredientes, el objetivo de las salsas es realzar el sabor del plato principal.

Algunas necesitan días para preparar, otras se pueden hacer en segundos...

Los clientes de EL PIANO nos han adorado durante muchos años por nuestras salsas iy algunos dicen que vienen solo por los chutneys!

Standard chutneys from garden produce are based on one simple recipe...2 units of chopped fruit or vegetable, such as apples or tomatoes, 1 unit of chopped onions, 1 unit of sugar and ¼ unit of vinegar. The spices are entirely to taste.

Cook the mix until it reduces so that the fluid gels when touching a cool surface such as a plate or marble. Pour into jars. Generally this chutney will keep indefinitely in the fridge. If you wish to store it in pickling jars, fill each jar to the line indicated. Seal the lid. Submerge the jars in cold water and bring to the boil. As the water heats up bubbles of air will escape the jar but no water will enter, thus creating a vacuum. This increases the unrefrigerated storage time to years.

Chutneys normales usando productos de la huerta están basados en una sola y sencilla receta...2 unidades de fruta o verdura picada, como manzanas o tomates, 1 unidad de cebolla picada, 1 unidad de azúcar y ¼ unidad de vinagre. Especias al gusto.

Cocinar. Cuando el líquido se gelifique al tocar una superficie fría como el mármol, verter en tarros. Debería durar indefinitivamente en el frigorífico. Si quiere guardarlo en tarros sin frío, llenar tarros de preservación hasta la linea indicada. Cerrar. Sumergir en agua fría y hervir. Cuando el agua se calienta las burbujas escapan del tarro pero el agua no entra. Se crea un vacío. Se puede guardar los tarros años fuera del frigorífico en un lugar seco.

in TOMATO chutney we use sweet & spicy paprika, mustard seeds, root ginger - for APPLE chutney we add coriander & mustard seeds & raisins
las especias que usamos para el chutney de **TOMATE** son mostaza, pimentón dulce y picante y jengibre - para el chutney de **MANZANA** usamos cilantro, mostaza y pasas

15

lime pickle   pickle de lima

Fill a 2L *pickling jar* with chopped *limes*. Turn into a bowl and rub with 1 TBL of *sea salt*. Stuff them back in the jar. Seal. Leave to sweat. Turn jar from time to time.

After 3 weeks tip out and add 1 tsp each of *mustard*, *fenugreek*, *cumin* seeds, 8 chopped *red chilles* and a pinch of *turmeric*. Back in the jar... Wait another 3-5 days while the lime skins soften.

Finally, dry-fry mustard seeds and add with 200ml of *olive oil*. Store in a cool place, the longer the better.

Llenar un **tarro** de 2L con **limas** picadas. Verter en una fuente y añadir 1 CDA de **sal marina**. Mezclar bien. Guardar en el tarro. Tapar. Dejar 3 semanas para que las limas suden y suelten su zumo. Voltear tarro de vez en cuando.

Verter otra vez en una fuente y añadir 1 cdt de semillas de **mostaza**, **fenogreco** y **comino**, 8 **guindillas rojas** picadas y una pizca de **cúrcuma**. Guardar en el tarro. Esperar 3-5 días hasta que las limas se ablanden.

Por último, sofreír en una sartén seca 1 CDA de semillas de mostaza y añadir con 200ml de **aceite de oliva**. Almacenar en un lugar frío, cuanto más tiempo mejor.

todo bajo en colesterol
all low cholesterol

For CILANTRO **whizz 4 units of** tofu, **1 unit of** olive oil. **Add fresh** coriander, garlic, lime juice **and** salt **to taste.**

*Para CILANTRO batir 4 unidades de **tofu** con 1 unidad de **aceite de oliva**. Añadir **cilantro fresco**, **ajo**, zumo de **lima** y **sal** al gusto.*

For MAYO **whizz 4 units of** tofu **with 1 unit of** olive oil. **Add** lemon juice **and** salt **to taste.**

*Para MAYO batir 4 unidades de **tofu** con 1 unidad de **aceite de oliva**. Añadir **zumo de limón** y **sal** al gusto.*

For RAITHA **grate 2** cucumbers, **squeezing out the juice. Whizz 500ml of** soya milk **with** vinegar **and** sugar **to taste and 3 stalks of fresh** mint. **Add the cucumber.**

*Para RAITHA rallar 2 **pepinos**, estrujar para sacar jugo. Batir 500ml de **leche de soja** con las hojas de 3 ramas de **hierbabuena**, vinagre y **azúcar** al gusto. Añadir el pepino.*

mango chutney (apricots or persimmons can be used too...)
chutney de mango (se puede usar albaricoques o caquis también...)

Esterilizar 6 **tarros** de 500ml. Mezclar en un bol 3K de **mangos** pelados y cortados (con huesos pesan 4,5K+) con 1,5K de **azúcar**. Dejar un día. El próximo día pelar y picar 1,5K de **cebollas**, rallar 200g de **ajo** y 200g de **jengibre**. Mezclar con los mangos y azúcar y cocinar lentamente. Mientras, sofreír en una sartén seca 1 cdt de cada especia en grano: **comino, cilantro, cardamomo, clavo** y en polvo: **pimienta cayena** y **cúrcuma**. Añadir a los mangos. Por último echar 750ml de **vinagre** de vino blanco. Cocinar 3 horas lentamente hasta que el chutney espese y cuaje cuando está frío. Verter en los tarros, cerrar y guardar en un lugar frío.

Sterilise 6 500ml jars. Put 3K of peeled, chopped and stoned mangos in a bowl (with stones weighing 4.5K+) with 1.5K of sugar. Leave overnight.

The next day peel and chop 1.5K onions, grate 200g of garlic and 200g of fresh ginger. Mix with the mangos and sugar and cook slowly. Meanwhile dry fry 1 tsp each of whole: cumin, coriander, cardomom, cloves and 1 tsp each of powdered cayenne and powdered turmeric. Add to the mangos. Finally add 750ml of white wine vinegar. Cook slowly for 3 hours or until the chutney thickens and sets when cold. Pour into the jars, seal and store in a cool place.

Un relish sencillo de una receta de mi familia del siglo 17...

Cortar en lonchas 4 unidades de pepinos y 1 unidad de cebollas. Hervir 1 unidad de azúcar con ¼ unidad de agua y ½ unidad de vinagre. Añadir eneldo seco, 1 cdt por litro de liquido, o 4 ramas frescas por litro de líquido, y sal al gusto. Verter encima de los pepinos y cebollas. Guardar en el frigorífico en tarros o en un bol.

A really simple relish recipe from my family from the 1600s...

Slice 4 units of cucumber to 1 unit of sliced onions. Boil 1 unit of sugar with ¼ unit of water and ½ unit of vinegar. Per litre of fluid add either 1 tsp of dry dill or 4 stalks of fresh and salt to taste. Pour over the cucumber and the onions. Keep in the fridge in jars or in a bowl.

salsas basadas en tomate
tomato based sauces

The photograph shows **LLAJUA** de Bolivia, a piquant sauce of whizzed tomatoes, garlic, chillies, mint, olive oil and salt. All quantities to taste.

La foto es de **LLAJUA** *de Bolivia, una salsa picante. Batir tomates, ajo, guindillas, hierbabuena, aceite de oliva y sal. Todas las cantidades al gusto.*

Para **SALSA de FUEGO** sofreír 2 **guindillas rojas** picadas en **aceite de oliva** con 1 **cebolla** picada. Añadir 250ml de **tomate frito**. Añadir **sal** al gusto y batir.

For **FIRE SAUCE** *fry 2 chopped red chillies in olive oil with 1 chopped onion. Add 175ml of tomato paste and 75ml of water. Whizz and add salt to taste.*

FENNEL SAUCE
is 100ml olive oil, 10 quartered tomatoes, 1 chopped onion, 2 tsp of fennel seeds, 1 head of chopped fennel, 1 tsp salt, 1 TBL sugar. Cover and cook slowly. The juices will make the sauce. After 20 mins, remove from the heat, whizz and add chopped fresh basil.

SALSA HINOJO
es 100ml de aceite de oliva, 10 tomates cortados en cuartos, 1 cebolla picada, 2 cdt de semillas de hinojo, 1 cabeza de hinojo picado, 1 cdt de sal, 1 CDA de azúcar. Tapar y cocinar lentamente. Los jugos hacen la salsa...Después de 20 mins quitar del fuego. Batir y añadir albahaca fresca.

KETCHUP...
...is best made using tomato concentrate. Fry gently with a little olive oil, cinnamon, sugar, salt & vinegar. Quantities to taste...

...es mejor si usamos tomate concentrado. Si no, usar tomate frito. Sofreír lentamente con aceite de oliva, canela, azúcar, sal y vinagre. Cantidades al gusto...

La salsa tai es fabulosa para aliñar ensaladas, dar sabor a tallarines o simplemente para mojar frituras, y encima, es muy sencilla de preparar. Sofreír 1 cebolla picada en aceite vegetal con 1 guindilla roja picada y 3 rodajas de jengibre. Añadir 1L de agua y 200g de crema de coco. Hervir con una hoja de lima. Añadir sal al gusto.

Thai sauce is fab for dressing salads, flavouring noodles or simply as a dip for fritters. What's more it's easy to make. Chop 1 onion, 1 red chilli and 3 slices of ginger and sautée in vegetable oil. Boil with 1L of water, 200g of creamed coconut & a lime leaf. Add salt to taste.

una salsa gravy tradicional combina la grasa y el jugo de carne con el agua usada para cocinar las verduras - como tal el gravy es una comida nutritiva en sí - ¡quizás esta versión es mejor!

traditional gravy combines meat juices and fats with water discarded from boiled vegetables - as such it is a nutritious meal in its own right - perhaps our version is even better...

To make 2L of gravy fry a chopped onion in 3 TBL olive oil until golden. As with bechamel, remove from heat & stir in 3 TBL of flour (gram/buckwheat/rice). Return to heat & add 2L of liquid, which can be water, stock or red wine, or a combination of the three. Cook until thickened. Salt & darken the colour with miso, tamari or Marmite to taste.

Para hacer 2L de gravy sofreír 1 cebolla picada en 3 CDA de aceite de oliva hasta que la cebolla se dore. Como la salsa bechamel, quitar del fuego y añadir 3 CDA de harina (garbanzo/sarraceno/arroz). Cocinar y añadir 2L de líquido que puede ser agua, caldo o vino tinto, o una combinación de los tres. Seguir cocinando hasta que el gravy espese. Sazonar y dar un toque marron con miso, tamari o Marmite al gusto.

cebollas onions

This onion relish is almost instant... Peel and chop 1 purple onion and rub in 1 tsp salt. Leave five minutes and chop 8 mint leaves. Squeeze the liquid out of the onions and add the mint, then 2 tsp sugar and 1 tsp white wine vinegar. Ready!

*Se puede hacer este relish de cebollas casi al instante... Pelar y picar 1 **cebolla morada** y mezclar con 1 cdt de **sal**. Dejar aparte. Mientras, picar 6 hojas de **hierbabuena**. Estrujar las cebollas para sacar el jugo y añadir la hierbabuena, 2 cdt de **azúcar** y 1 cdt de **vinagre de vino blanco**. ¡Listo!*

una mermelada de cebollas muy sencilla y sin grasa...
cortar 1K de cebollas y combinar solo con 2 CDA de azúcar moreno y sal al gusto. Sofreír al fuego lento en una sartén. Cuando las cebollas estén transparentes la mermelada está lista.

simple onion marmalade without fat...
chop 1K onions. Fry gently in 2 TBL brown sugar & salt to taste. When translucent the marmalade is ready.

Todo el mundo piensa que hacer sopas y cremas es fácil, y lo es. Pero ese toque especial que atrae a personas desde la otra punta de la ciudad en días de lluvia y frío, eso es otra cosa...

Estas recetas estan inspiradas por l@s grandes cociner@s de El Piano. Mike Brid estuvo 2 años en York, Elaina todavía está allí y Mayra estuvo en Granada desde el principio. (En Málaga, suele hacer demasiado calor para sopas.)

El secreto es usar pocos ingredientes de primera calidad y crear una armonía perfecta entre ellas y las hierbas y especias. Si usamos demasiadas hierbas o especias su sabor domina, y si usamos pocas falta algo...

Cada cociner@ tiene su toque especial y en estas recetas los explican.

tomates y hierbas ecológicos
organic tomatoes & herbs
LA HUERTA SANTA MARÍA, GRANADA
dueña/owner Sacri López
agricultor/grower Inocencio Ortega Naranjo

It is commonly believed that soup-making is easy. And indeed it is. But soups that make people walk across a city in poor weather to buy them...they are something else...

These recipes are inspired by the great soup-makers of EL PIANO. Mike Brid who spent two years in York, Elaina who is still there, and Mayra who was in Granada from the start. (Most of the time it's too warm in Málaga for soup.)

Usually we use a few first class quality ingredients in a perfect harmony along with a mastery of herbs and spices. Too much, and that's all that is tasted, too little, and the palate yearns for more.

Every cook has their own special touch and in these recipes they explain theirs.

carrot & coriander   zanahoria y cilantro

*Reckon 2 carrots and ½ onion per person.
Chop them coarsely.
Sautée in olive oil with pinch of salt per person.
Coarsely chop fresh coriander, one full leafy stalk
per person, and set aside.*

*Keep the lid on the pan and continue to sweat the
veg on a low heat. When they are golden and the
carrots tender, add water just short of covering
them. Continue to cook until the carrots break up.*

*Remove from the heat. Whizz. Adjust salt to
taste. If too thick, add water. Return to the heat.
When the soup is boiling throw in the coriander,
put the lid on and turn off the heat.
Wait 5 mins.
Serve.*

Calcular 2 **zanahorias** y ½ **cebolla** por persona. Cortarlas en trozos grandes.

Sofreír en **aceite de oliva** y **sal** con 1 cdt de aceite y una pizca de sal por persona. Picar una rama de **cilantro fresco** por persona y guardar aparte.

Bajar el fuego y mantener la olla tapada. Cuando las verduras estén doradas y las zanahorias tiernas, añadir agua hasta que estén casi cubiertas. Seguir cocinando hasta que las zanahorias se deshagan. Quitar del fuego. Batir. Añadir sal al gusto y más agua si hace falta. Volver al fuego. Cuando hierva, echar el cilantro picado. Tapar la olla. Quitar del fuego y dejar reposar 5 mins. Servir.

courgette/marrow soup   crema de calabacín

una crema que se puede tomar fría o caliente. las semillas de los calabacines grandes dan un toque muy sabroso

a soup that can be enjoyed hot or cold. the seeds from the larger mature marrows add an especially good flavour

En una olla sofreír calabacines cortados con cebolla y ajo (opcional) en aceite de oliva. Echar un poco de sal y pimenta negra. Cuando las verduras estén doradas cubrir con agua. Tapar la olla, bajar el fuego y dejar cocinar lentamente hasta que las verduras estén blandas. Batir. Añadir más sal al gusto. Por último, añadir un surtido de hierbas frescas picadas como perejil, albahaca, cilantro, hierbabuena... Las cantidades de los ingredientes son al gusto. Se puede congelar.

In a pan sautée chopped courgettes/marrows with onion and garlic (optional) in olive oil. Add a little salt and pepper. When golden cover with water and a lid and reduce the heat. Cook slowly until the vegetables are tender. Remove from the heat. Whizz. Add salt to taste. Finally throw in an assortment of fresh herbs such as parsley, basil, mint or coriander. Quantities according to your preferences. Easily frozen.

una oportunidad excelente para usar los calabacines del jardín o balcón isobre todo cuando hay muchos!

an excellent opportunity to use courgettes or marrows from the garden or the balcony, especially when there are a lot of them!

chowder de maíz   corn chowder

A soup in 2 parts for 4 people.

Boil 8 cubed potatoes and 1 TBL of sage in 500ml of water until soft.

Prepare a version of bechamel sauce: sauté a diced onion in 3 TBL olive oil. When translucent remove from the heat. Add 3 TBL buckwheat flour taking care that the flour is absorbed fully by the oil before returning to the heat. Little by little add 500ml white wine, stirring constantly until the bechamel thickens.

Add 200g soya cream cheese and then whizz the sauce with the potatoes, sage and their water.

Finally add 200g corn kernels and salt to taste.

Una sopa en 2 partes para 4 personas.

*Hervir 8 **patatas** cortadas y 1 CDA de **salvia** en 500ml de **agua** hasta que estén blandas.*

*Preparar una versión de salsa bechamel: sofreír 1 **cebolla** picada en 3 CDA de **aceite de oliva**. Cuando esté transparente quitar del fuego y añadir 3 CDA de **harina de sarraceno**. Asegurar que la harina absorba todo el aceite antes de volver a cocinar. Poco a poco añadir 500ml de **vino blanco** removiendo constantemente hasta que la bechamel espese.*

*Añadir 200g de **queso de soja para untar original** y batir la salsa con las patatas, la salvia y su agua.*

*Por último, añadir 200g de **maíz en grano** y **sal** al gusto.*

la clásica receta de sopa de miso es cebollas y zanahorias sofritas con agua, miso y col cocida al vapor, a veces cubitos de tofu flotan encima con trocitos de los tallos verdes de cebolleta
el miso es el resultado de un proceso de fermentación y es especialmente curativo - para preservar sus propiedades saludables es importante evitar hervirlo - el tipo de miso más común es el de soja, muy salado con un color oscuro
en nuestra receta usamos un miso más claro que deriva del arroz - aunque tradicionalmente no se permiten carbohidratos en las sopas de miso, nuestra versión esta basada en patatas

Hervir patatas y cebollas en agua hasta que estén blandas. Quitar del fuego. Batir con SHIRO miso al gusto.
Boil potatoes and onions in water until soft. Remove from the heat. Whizz and add SHIRO miso to taste.

this is the only personal remark in the recipes...MISO soup is probably my favourite soup of all time and, in either form, is the only soup I ever crave...

éste es el único comentario personal en las recetas...la sopa de MISO probablemente es mi preferida de todas - hecha de cualquier manera, es la única sopa que se me antoja...

traditional miso soup is sautéed onions and carrots, then water, miso and steamed cabbage, sometimes little cubes of tofu float on the top with diced spring onions
miso is the product of fermentation and is particularly curative - in order to maintain its health giving properties it is important to avoid boiling - the most common form is from soya beans and is very salty and dark in colour
our version uses a blonder miso derived from fermented rice - although traditionally the soup does not permit carbohydrates, our version is based on potatoes

27

field bean broth   crema marroquí

Poner 100g de habas secas en remojo el día anterior. Sofreír en 2 CDA de aceite de oliva, 1 cebolla picada y 10g de pimentón picante. Añadir las habas y 1,5L de agua. Hervir hasta que estén tiernas y se deshagan un poco. Añadir sal al gusto. Batir y servir adornada con perejil fresco.

*Soak 100g dried **field beans** overnight. Sauté 1 **onion** and 10g spicy **paprika** in 2 TBL olive oil. Add the broad beans and 1.5L of **water**. Boil until the beans are tender and starting to break up. **Salt** to taste. Whizz and serve topped with chopped **fresh parsley**.*

A typical simple Moroccan gruel with a delicate flavour...Experiment by adding sweet spices to contrast with the piquancy of the paprika. It is a particular EL PIANO favourite since the beans are rich in nutrients, easy to grow, yet usually fed to livestock.

Una "crema campesina" sencilla y típica de Marruecos, con un sabor muy delicado. Experimentar con especias dulces que contrasten con el picante del pimentón. Las habas son fáciles de cultivar, muy nutritivas, y, secas, solo se suelen usar para alimentar animales.

It is the only recipe that we repeat in...
Es la única receta que aparece también en...

DOSSIER - habas/field beans

ISBN 978-0-9563980-2-4

Para 4 personas.
*Picar 1 **cebolla** y sofreír en 100ml de **aceite de oliva**. Cuando esté dorada, añadir 500g de **guisantes congelados** y suficiente **agua** para cubrirlos. Tapar la olla, bajar el fuego y dejar cocinar lentamente durante 15 mins. Quitar del fuego. Batir. Añadir más agua si hace falta y **sal** al gusto.*

For 4 people.
Sauté 1 diced onion in 100ml olive oil. When golden, add 500g frozen peas and enough water to cover them. Cover the pan, reduce the heat and leave to cook slowly for 15 minutes. Remove from the heat. Whizz. Add more water if necessary. Salt to taste.

no hay otra crema más sencilla que ésta - sin embargo, el resultado siempre es espectacular...
there is no soup as simple as this one - nonetheless, the result is always spectacular...

Calcular por persona 1 **patata** cortada en lonchas, ½ **cebolla** cortada en media lunas, 1 CDA de **aceite de oliva**, 100ml de **vino tinto** y **sal** y **pimenta negra** al gusto.

Sofreír las patatas y cebolla en el aceite con una pizca de sal. Bajar el fuego y mantener la olla tapada. Cuando las verduras estén doradas y tiernas, añadir el vino. Bajar el fuego y seguir cocinando hasta que las patatas se deshagan. Quitar del fuego. Batir. Añadir agua hasta llegar a la consistencia deseada. Añadir sal al gusto y espolvorear la pimienta negra encima.

One portion of soup would be 1 sliced potato, ½ sliced onion, 1 TBL olive oil, 100ml red wine. Salt and black pepper to taste.

Sauté the potates and onion in the oil with a pinch of salt. Reduce the heat and keep the pan covered. When the vegetables are tender, add the wine and continue cooking on a low heat. When the potatoes are breaking up remove from the heat and whizz. If too thick, add water. Adjust salt to taste and sprinkle black pepper on top.

Poor quality wine that tastes like kerosene will result in poor quality soup that tastes like kerosene. Use quality.

Cuanto más bueno sea el vino utilizado, mejor será el sabor de la crema. Usar vino de buena calidad.

Soup for 4: 1 entire head (a corn) of garlic, 16 large tomatoes, 500g spinach, 1 TBL olive oil, 1 200-300g tin of red kidney beans or equivalent cooked beans

*Sopa para 4 personas: 1 cabeza de **ajo**, 16 **tomates** grandes, 500g de **espinacas**, 1 CDA de **aceite de oliva**, 200-300g de **alubias rojas** cocidas*

Wash, chop and toss all of the ingredients, EXCEPT the beans, in a pan with the oil and a pinch of **salt**. Cover the pan and leave on a low heat until the juices have left the veg. Remove from the heat. Add salt to taste, water if required, and the beans.

Lavar, picar y echar todos los ingredientes, EXCEPTO las alubias, en una olla con el aceite y una pizca de sal. Tapar y dejar cocinar lentamente hasta que el jugo salga de las verduras. Quitar del fuego. Añadir sal al gusto, agua si es necesario, y las alubias.

parece mucho ajo...pero no lo es...el sabor del ajo disminuye cuando se hierva y es muy delicado

it seems like a lot of garlic... but it isn't...the flavour of garlic reduces during boiling and is very delicate

white winter warmer   sopa de invierno

Reckon 2 parsnips, 1 potato, ½ onion and 50g of butter beans per person. Soak the beans the day before, drain and cook, ideally in a pressure cooker, until soft. Drain, saving the water.

Chop the vegetables coarsely. Sauté them in 1 tsp olive oil and a pinch of salt per person.

Keep the lid on the pan and continue to sweat the veg on a low heat.

When they are tender, add the bean water just short of covering them. Continue to cook until they break up. Remove from the heat. Whizz. If too thick, add water. Add the beans. Adjust salt to taste. Serve.

Calcular 2 **chirivías**, 1 **patata**, ½ **cebolla** y 50g de **alubias blancas grandes** por persona.

Poner las alubias en remojo el día antes. Escurrirlas y cocinar en una **olla de presión** si es posible, hasta que estén blandas. Escurrir, guardando el agua.

Cortar las verduras en trozos grandes. Sofreír en 1 cdt de **aceite de oliva** y una pizca de **sal** por persona.

Bajar el fuego y dejar la olla tapada. Cuando las verduras estén tiernas, añadir el agua de las alubias hasta casi cubrir las verduras.

Seguir cocinando hasta que las verduras se deshagan. Quitar del fuego. Batir. Añadir las alubias cocidas, sal al gusto y más agua si hace falta. Servir.

L@s cociner@s de EL PIANO suelen ser de todas partes del mundo, la mayoría de ell@s trabajan con nosotros durante años. No es sorprendente entonces que la cocina de EL PIANO esté en desarrollo constante.

Esta sección del libro es una mezcla de recetas ordenadas en pequeños capítulos para poder encontrarlas rápidamente.

Hemos añadido algunas recetas que se han desarrollado desde MANO a MANO (el libro de los platos salados de EL PIANO) e incluido recetas imprescindibles como pan, masa de panadería y tofu.

Si tiene alguna duda o pregunta sobre las recetas contacte con nosotros por email.

También ofrecemos clases de cocina cada año, en Inglaterra y en España, por si quiere participar y divertirse.
Algunas de ellas son gratis.

With so many cooks, some of whom stay with us years, and with so many of them from different cultures and traditions it is hardly surprising that the EL PIANO kitchen is in a state of constant evolution.

This section includes a variety of recipes that we have put into sub-sections for ease of reference. Essentially we are updating and augmenting the savoury recipes developed since HANDING IT ON and also including indispensible staples such as bread, pastry and tofu.

If you have any doubts or questions about the recipes do contact us by email.

Additionally if you wish to join us for some face to face fun, we have a series of classes that are offered each year, both in Spain and in the UK. Some of these events are free of charge.

PAN - *BREAD*

FRITURAS
FRITTERS

TO*FU*

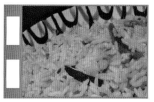

ARROZ - *RICE*

MI*SC*

33

pan   bread

con levadura en polvo
with baking powder

con levadura madre
with yeast

sin levadura
unleavened

con bicarbonato de sodio
with baking soda

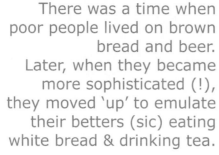

There was a time when poor people lived on brown bread and beer. Later, when they became more sophisticated (!), they moved 'up' to emulate their betters (sic) eating white bread & drinking tea.

Either way, this vital carbohydrate is a staple. And it's a useful vehicle to get stuff into your mouth... For people unable to eat gluten it can be difficult. Here are 4 options:

A bread made with corn and BAKING POWDER, still popular in the Americas... A YEASTED version common in Europe... An UNLEAVENED BREAD, the simplest of all, which we find in varying forms world-wide... SODA BREAD, long traditional in Ireland and Wales...

Some are faster to make than others but all are excellent candidates for the freezer and none contains gluten or animal products.

Hace años la gente pobre se alimentaba con pan integral y cerveza.
Luego se consideraba más sofisticado (!) comer pan blanco, un producto refinado, como hacía la gente rica.

De cualquier manera, este carbohidrato fundamental aparece en casi todas las dietas. Y, es un vehículo muy útil para transportar comida a la boca. Para las personas que no pueden comer gluten es difícil. Hay 4 opciones:

Pan hecho de maíz y LEVADURA EN POLVO, *todavía popular en las Américas...*
Pan de LEVADURA MADRE, *la versión común de Europa...*
Pan SIN LEVADURA, *el más sencillo de todos, que se encuentra en todo el mundo...*
Pan irlandés con BICARBONATO DE SODIO...

Algunos son más rápidos de hacer que otros, pero todos se pueden congelar y ninguno lleva gluten ni productos animales.

preheat oven to
precalentar el horno a
150°C

Mix 350g cornmeal or polenta with 100g sugar, 25g baking powder, 100 ml sunflower oil & a pinch of salt.
Add 800ml boiling water and stir thoroughly but quickly. Pour into a 1L oiled oven tray and bake at 150°C for 10-15 mins. When cool, cut into squares.

*Mezclar 350g de **sémola de maíz**, 100g de **azúcar**, 25g de **levadura en polvo**, 100ml de **aceite de girasol** y una pizca de **sal**.*
*Añadir 800ml de **agua hirviendo** y remover bien pero rápido.*
*Verter en una **bandeja de horno** de 1L y hornear a 150°C durante 10-15 mins. Dejar hasta que se enfríe y cortar en cuadrados.*

cornbread was traditionally the bread of the American cowboy - by throwing the mix into the empty bacon pan to absorb the fat, it also cleaned it - it's easy to add herbs, onions, or vegetables to this bread or equally toss in raisins and coconut

el pan de maíz fue el pan tradicional de los vaqueros americanos - el acto de poner la masa en la sartén del beicon hacía que absorbía la grasa y, al mismo tiempo, dejaba la sartén limpia - se puede añadir hierbas, cebollas o verduras cocidas e, incluso, pasas y coco

panecitos rolls

preheat oven to 170°C - *precalentar el horno a 170°C*
put a pan of water to boil - *poner una olla de agua a hervir*

Mix 350g **rice flour**, 700g **buckwheat flour**, 100g **sugar**, 25g **xantham gum** & a pinch of **salt**. Mix in 25g of **dried yeast**. Add herbs & seeds to taste as an optional extra.

*Mezclar 350g de **harina de arroz**, 700g de **harina de sarraceno**, 100g de **azúcar**, 25g de **goma xantana** y una pizca de **sal**. Añadir 25g de **levadura madre** seca y mezclar. Añadir hierbas o semillas al gusto (opcional).*

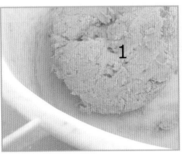

1. Add 800ml blood-hot **water** to make a dough.
*1. Añadir 800ml **agua** tibia (temperatura de sangre) y hacer la masa.*

2. Form bun-sized balls. Press on **silicone baking sheet** on an oven tray.
*2. Aplastar bolitas encima de un **salvabandejas** de silicona en una bandeja de horno.*

3. Place over pan of boiling water. Cover in a **cloth**.
*3. Colocar la bandeja encima de la olla de agua hirviendo y cubrir con un **trapo**.*

4. When double in size bake 10-15 mins.
4. Cuando el pan haya doblado su tamaño, hornear 10-15 mins.

the EASIEST thing ever...three year olds can get involved... simply add water to 500g buckwheat flour and a pinch of salt - make the batter the thickness you prefer - a runny mix will yield 80 blinis - a little oil in the mix will prevent them sticking - herbs, sugar, spices, fresh fruit and pure vanilla are wonderful variations...simply drop like mini pancakes on a griddle or frying pan

ésta es una receta tan sencilla que los niños de tres años también pueden involucrarse...simplemente añadir agua a 500g de harina de sarraceno y una pizca de sal hasta que la masa tenga la consistencia deseada. De una mezcla muy líquida salen 80 blinis. Echar un poco de aceite para que no se pegue a la sartén. Añdir hierbas, azúcar fruta fresca, especias o vainilla pura para variaciones deliciosas...cocinar a la plancha como mini crêpes o en una sartén

scones

Preheat oven to 170°C. Crumb 350g rice flour, 175g buckwheat flour, 175g muscovado sugar, 25g xantham gum, 30g baking soda or baking powder with 175g margarine and a pinch of salt. Add 250ml of 'milk' to make the dough. Finally add 175g raisins. Either roll out on a floured surface and cut into circles or form balls and flatten onto a silicone baking sheet.
Bake 15-20 mins.

Precalentar el horno a 170°C. Mezclar 350g de harina de arroz, 175g de harina de sarraceno, 175g de azúcar moreno, 25g de goma xantana, 30g de bicarbonato de sodio o levadura en polvo con 175g margarina y una pizca de sal. Añadir 250ml de 'leche' para crear una masa. Por último añadir 175g de pasas. Estirar la masa sobre una superficie bien enharinada y cortar en círculos o formar bolitas y aplastar encima de un salvabandejas de silicona.
Hornear 15-20 mins.

Practicamente cualquier verdura picada, sazonada y mezclada con cualquier tipo de harina y agua, puede crear una buena fritura. Una fritura clásica es el bhaji de Pakistán, una de las recetas favoritas de los clientes de EL PIANO - se encuentra en nuestro libro MANO a MANO. Algunas pautas para hacer frituras son:

...añadir suficiente sal. La grasa domina el sabor y, sin suficiente sal, las frituras pueden tener el sabor de grasa y solo de grasa.

...colocar las bolitas de masa en el aceite cuidadosamente y cerca de la superficie SIN dejarlas caer para que no salpique el aceite.

...se puede congelar las frituras. La mejor forma es freírlas parcialmente y congelar. Una vez que las quiere comer se pueden freír directamente del congelador o meter al horno para reducir consumo de grasa.

...echar sal a las verduras un par de horas antes de añadir la harina - el jugo de las verduras sale y hace falta menos agua.

...usar aceite vegetal para freír. Nunca usar aceite de oliva a menos que esté refinado. No se puede calentar el aceite de oliva virgen extra lo suficiente sin que se queme y las frituras absorben demasiada grasa.

Virtually any vegetable chopped, seasoned and mixed with any flour and water will make for a good fritter. The classic fritter is the bhaji from Pakistan which is in our book of savouries, HANDING IT ON. A few key bits of information about fritters are:

...the mix needs plenty of salt. Frying takes away from the general flavour and without more salt the fritter can simply taste of grease.

...place the fritter mix gently in the hot fat close to the surface. If you drop it in, the oil may splash.

...fritters can be frozen. Par-fry them. When you are ready to eat them, they can be fried from frozen or, to reduce fat intake, they can be finished in the oven.

...salt the vegetables a few hours before adding the flour - the juices of the vegetables will then reduce the water needed.

...use vegetable oil. Virgin olive oil will not reach a high enough temperature without smoking and the fritters will absorb too much fat.

pestolitos & pakoras

Pakoras

Chop a selection of seasonal vegetables, except onions, into chip-sized pieces (potatoes, cabbage, carrot, broccoli...). Think in terms of 100g of vegetables per person. Par boil hard vegetables, drain and add soft vegetables (peas, peppers, mushrooms...). Add salt, curry powder, cumin seeds and chopped fresh coriander to taste. Add chickpea flour (gram/garbanzo bean flour) & water to make a dough. Form into balls and deep fry in vegetable oil.

Cortar en tiras gruesas una selección de verduras de temporada, excepto cebolla (patatas, col, zanahoria, brócoli...). Calcular 100g de verduras por persona. Hervir verduras duras, escurrir y añadir verduras más blandas (guisantes, pimiento...). Añadir sal, curry en polvo, semillas de comino y cilantro fresco picado al gusto. Añadir harina de garbanzos y agua para crear una masa. Formar bolitas y freír en abundante aceite vegetal.

Batir un manojo de espinacas frescas con ½ manojo de albahaca fresca. Cortar 6 champiñones en láminas y picar 4 tomates en trozos. Mezclar todo con sal al gusto. Añadir harina de arroz para crear una masa. Formar tortitas y freír en abundante aceite vegetal.

Whizz a bag of **fresh spinach** with ½ the volume of **fresh basil**. Chop 4 **tomatoes** and slice 6 **mushrooms**. Mix all together and **salt** to taste. Add **rice flour** to make a dough. Form into patties and deep fry in **vegetable oil**.

Pestolitos

pakoras son la versión de la India de bhajis de Pakistán, pestolitos son nuestra versión europea...
pakoras are the Indian version of bhajis from Pakistan, pestolitos are our European version...

röstis y piña frita   röstis & fried pineapple

röstis son nada más que patatas ralladas y fritas - la clave es añadir un toque especial: hierbas como orégano, pimienta negra, y, a veces, queso de soja, cebolla o cebolleta

röstis are nothing more than grated and fried potatoes - the key is adding to the mix herbs like oregano, black pepper, and, at times, soya cheese, onions or spring onions

Pelar una piña fresca, cortarla en 2, cabeza a cola, y en rodajas de medias lunas. Mezclar una masa de 250g de harina de garbanzos, una pizca de sal, curry en polvo al gusto y 100ml de agua. Rebozar cada rodaja de piña en la masa y freír en abundante aceite vegetal.

Prepare a fresh pineapple. Cut in half, top to bottom & slice in half moons. Mix a batter of 250g chickpea flour (gram/garbanzo bean flour), a pinch of salt, curry powder to taste and 100ml water. Dip the pineapple pieces in the batter. Deep fry in vegetable oil.

Usar 1 patata grande por persona. Rallarlas, lavar y escurrir para quitar el almidón. Añadir sal al gusto y harina de patatas o harina de arroz y mezclar hasta crear una masa. Formar tortitas. Hay 2 opciones: freírlas en abundante aceite vegetal o, para usar menos grasa, cocinarlas a la plancha.

Choose a good-sized potato per person. Grate and rinse off the starch. Drain. Add salt to taste and potato or rice flour to make a dough. Shape into patties. There are 2 options. Deep fry in vegetable oil or, use less grease and flatten onto a griddle.

don't be tempted to use tinned pineapple - it is too sweet - it is the combination of the sweet and tart of fresh that makes this dish...

no caer en la tentación de usar piña de lata - es demasiado dulce - el éxito del plato es la combinación de ácido y dulce de piña fresca...

barquillos de tortillas   tortilla cups

Los papadums y las tortillas de maíz son las únicas cosas que no elaboramos nosotros. Compramos tortillas de maíz de Nagual en Barcelona. Fijar una tortilla entre dos tamices pequeños. Freír en abundante aceite vegetal hasta que se dore. Sacar y llenar con cualquier relleno...

Papadums and corn tortillas are the only things that we do not make ourselves. We buy the corn tortillas from Nagual in Barcelona. Fix a corn tortilla between two large tea strainers/small sieves. Deep fry until golden. Fill with whatever...

corn tortillas are easier to handle if warm
las tortillas de maíz son más fáciles de manipular cuando están calentitas

Elegir por persona 1 calabacín, ½ cebolla morada, ½ rama de eneldo, 2 hojas de menta y 1 cdt de zumo de limón. Rallar los calabacines y echar sal. Apretar para quitar el líquido. Añadir los demás ingredientes picados y suficiente harina de arroz para crear una masa. Formar tortitas. Freír en abundante aceite vegetal.

Choose 1 courgette, ½ purple onion, ½ stalk of dill, 2 mint leaves and 1 tsp lemon juice per person. Grate the courgettes. Add salt and press out the liquid. Add the other chopped ingredients plus rice flour to make a dough. Shape into balls and flatten. Deep fry in vegetable oil.

Las tinas de Bolivia son sencillas de hacer. Rallar zanahorias y picar la misma cantidad de cebolletas, pero solo la parte verde. Añadir sal y azúcar al gusto. Echar harina de arroz para crear una masa. Formar bolitas y freír en abundante aceite vegetal.

Tinas are a Bolivian recipe & super easy. Grate a quantity of **carrots** and chop the same quantity of **spring onions** (scallions). Add **salt** and **sugar** to taste. Add **rice flour** to make a dough. Form patties and deep fry in **vegetable oil**.

la salsa LLAJUA (p20) da un toque picante a las tinas y el sabor del tomate complementa el dulce de las zanahorias - el vinagre de la salsa ROANNE (p19) contrarresta la grasa de las calitas

LLAJUA (p20) lends a touch of piquancy to the tinas and the tomato complements the sweetness of the carrots - the vinegar in the ROANNE pickle (p19) counteracts the grease of the calitas

tofu

Use in salads, burgers and quiches as well as sautéed. Tofu has little flavour of its own and benefits from herbs, spices and other condiments. Eaten raw or cooked, tofu is a cholesterol-free protein alternative. Keep cool and submerged in clean water. Tofu does not freeze well.

Se puede usar tofu en ensaladas, hamburguesas, tartaletas y a la plancha. El tofu no tiene mucho sabor propio así que es mejor echarle hierbas, especias y otros condimentos. Crudo o cocido, el tofu es una proteína alternativa sin colesterol. Guardar en frío y sumergido en agua limpia. No se congela bien.

Cubitos de tofu crudo o ligeramente sofrito marinado en el zumo y ralladura de limas, con guindillas rojas picadas, ajo picado, cebolla roja en tiras finas, cilantro fresco picado y sal. Cantidades al gusto. Servir frío. ¡Todo un triunfo!

Cubes of raw or lightly sautéed tofu marinated in lime juice and grated lime peel with finely chopped red chillies, finely chopped garlic, finely sliced red onion, chopped fresh coriander and salt. Use quantities to taste. Serve cold. A triumph!

hacer tofu

despite all the pictures, which may seem off-putting, tofu is easy to make
a pesar de tantas fotos y explicaciones, el tofu es fácil de hacer

Comprar o hacer una prensa. En EL PIANO usamos 2 **cajas de verduras** iguales para 14L. Buscar cajas más pequeñas para uso doméstico. Cortar la base de una para crear **la 'bandeja gota'** y **la tapa**. Poner la 'bandeja gota' en una bandeja. Forrar la otra caja con **tela fina** que se usa para hacer 'queso fresco' y dejarla encima de **una rejilla** encima del fregadero.

*Buy or make a press. In EL PIANO we use 2 identical **crates** to make 14L. Look for smaller crates for domestic use. Cut the base from one to make the **drip tray** and also the weight **grid**. Put the drip tray on a tray. Line the other with **cheesecloth** and place over an **oven rack** across the sink.*

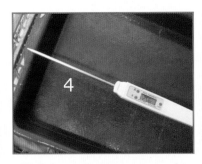  

Elegir un **plato pesado** y tener el **termómetro** a mano.
*Choose a **heavy dish** and have the **thermometer** to hand.*

Comprar **leche de soja pura** y ecológica. Hervir 5 mins. Quitar del fuego.
*Buy **organic soya milk** without additives. Boil 5 mins. Remove from heat.*

Pesar la **sal nigari** (sal mineral de Japón) 10g por litro de leche.
*Weigh the **nigari** (Japanese mineral salt) 10g per litre of milk.*

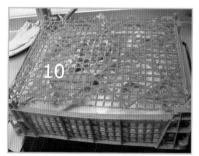

Cuando la leche esté 70°-80°C añadir la sal. Remover 1 sola vez. La leche coagulará. Dejar reposar 20 mins.
When the milk is 70°-80°C add the salt. Stir once. The milk will coagulate. Leave it to rest 20 minutes

Con cuidado meter la leche coagulada dentro de la caja forrada de tela.
Carefully put the coagulated milk in the cheesecloth-lined crate.

Doblar la tela sobrante para cubrir el tofu.
Fold the cloth edges to cover the tofu.

Colocar la tapa encima.
Put the grid on top.

Poner el plato pesado encima.
Weight it with the heavy plate.

Poner la caja encima de la 'bandeja gota' en el frigorífico 24 horas.
Place on drip tray & cool in the fridge 24 hours.

Store tofu submerged in water. Change the water periodically & it will last three weeks. Tofu does not generally freeze well.
Guardar el tofu sumergido en agua. Cambiar el agua de vez en cuando y dura 3 semanas. En general el tofu no se congela bien.

rice arroz

arroz redondo o arroz largo... arroz blanco o arroz integral...

long or short grain rice... white rice or brown...

PERFECT RICE EVERY TIME...

Boil 2 units of liquid per 1 unit of rice. Add the rice. Stir once and bring back to the boil. Stir again. Cover. Lower the heat. Wait 20 mins. It's ready!

Usually the liquid is water, but fruit juice can also be used. A great variation is orange juice with ginger and tamari or pineapple juice with wasabi...

ARROZ PERFECTO CADA VEZ

Hervir 2 unidades de líquido por cada 1 unidad de arroz. Añadir el arroz. Remover una vez y esperar hasta que el agua hierva de nuevo. Remover otra vez. Tapar. Bajar el fuego. Esperar 20 mins. ¡Está listo!

Normalmente el líquido es agua, pero se puede usar zumo también. Variaciones pueden ser zumo de naranja con jengibre y tamari o zumo de piña con wasabi...

aubergine rice & paella
arroz con berenjenas y paella

Para el arroz con berenjenas freír berenjenas en cubitos y dientes de ajo en aceite de oliva. Añadir al arroz ya cocido. Echar perejil picado, zumo de limón y tamari. Las cantidades son al gusto.

For aubergine rice fry cubed **aubergines** with **garlic** cloves in **olive oil**. Add to prepared **rice**. Throw in chopped **parsley**, **lemon juice** and **tamari**. The quantities of everything are up to you.

Las algas son lo que le da a nuestra paella su sabor del mar. Cocinar el arroz con hiziki y cúrcuma, 1 unidad de hiziki por cada 4 unidades de arroz y 1 cdt de cúrcuma por cada 500g de arroz. Dejarlo aparte. En una sartén sofreír en aceite de oliva, pimientos rojos y pimientos verdes picados, cebollas y cebolletas picadas, incluyendo las partes verdes. Mezclar las verduras con el arroz. Echar sal al gusto.

Seaweed gives our paella its marine taste. Cook 4 units of **rice** with 1 unit of **hiziki** and 1 tsp of **turmeric** per 500g of rice. Set aside. Separately, in **olive oil**, sauté **red** and **green peppers**, **onions** and **spring onions** (including the green tails). Mix the vegetables into the rice and **salt** to taste.

coconut rice & exotic rice
arroz de coco y arroz exótico

arroz exótico

el arroz es el único ingrediente peligroso en la cocina vegana - HAY que mantenerlo siempre a 5°-8°C
rice is the only dangerous ingredient in the vegan kitchen it MUST be stored cold, 5°-8°C

Cocinar el arroz pero, en vez de agua, usar leche de coco. Después, echar cualquier fruta fresca. En la foto abajo hemos usado cerezas.

Cook the rice but instead of water use **coconut milk**. Once cooked, add whatever **fresh fruit**. In the photo below we have used cherries.

Sofreír en **aceite vegetal** (no de oliva) 1 **cebolla**, 1 diente de **ajo** (opcional) y 1 cdt de cada especia en grano como: clavo, cardamomo, pimienta, comino, cilantro, mostaza, fenogreco y canela en rama. Añadir ½L de **arroz** (volumen) y sofreír todo junto 2 mins. Añadir 1L de **agua** salada. Hervir. Tapar. Bajar el fuego. Esperar 20 mins.

Sauté in vegetable oil 1 onion, 1 clove of garlic (optional) and 1 tsp each of whole spices, i.e. cloves, cardamoms, peppercorns, cumin, coriander, mustard, fenugreek and cinnamon sticks. Add ½L of rice (volume). Sauté 2 mins. Add 1L salted water. Boil. Cover. Reduce heat. Wait 20 mins.

arroz de coco

Los platos salados de El Piano salen en varios libros nuestros:

HAND to MOUTH (mano a boca) 2002
inglés
HAND in HAND (mano en mano) 2003
inglés
HANDING it ON - MANO a MANO 2009
inglés y español

Aquí hemos añadido un surtido de nuevas recetas saladas.
Hay algunas que representan nuevos cocineros en El Piano de América Latina, especialmente de Bolivia y de Perú.

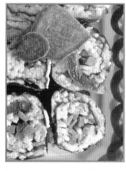

The savoury dishes of El Piano are in various of our cookbooks:

HAND to MOUTH, 2002
in English
HAND in HAND, 2003
in English
HANDING it ON - MANO a MANO 2009
in English and in Spanish

Here we add a selection of new savoury recipes. Some of them represent new cooks in El Piano, particularly from Latin America, especially Bolivia and Peru.

'boeuf' estragón 'boeuf' tarragon

Echar poco **aceite de oliva** en una **olla a presión** y sofreír 1 **puerro** picado, 12 **champiñones** en lonchas y 1 CDA de **estragón**. Añadir 100g de **soja texturizada gruesa**, 1L de **vino blanco** y una pizca de **sal**. Cocinar a presión 30 mins. Quitar del fuego. Dejar que la presión baje, abrir y servir.

Using little olive oil sauté in a pressure cooker 1-2 diced leeks, 12 sliced mushrooms and 1 TBL tarragon. Add 100g chunky soya (TVP), 1L white wine and a pinch of salt. Cook under pressure 30 mins. Remove from the heat. Allow the pressure to drop, open and serve.

'beef' stew   estofado

Sofreír 2 cebollas cortadas en cuadrados en aceite de oliva con 1 cdt de pimentón picante y 1 cdt de pimentón dulce. Añadir 4 zanahorias en rodajas. Añadir 50g de soja texturizada gruesa y un poco de sal. Sofreír hasta que la soja haya absorbido el aceite y las especias. Añadir 125ml de vino tinto y luego agua hasta que cubra todos los ingredientes. Dejar cocinar hasta que la soja y las zanahorias estén cocinadas.

Aparte, freír 2 patatas medianas en cuadrados en abundante aceite vegetal hasta que estén bien doradas.

Añadir las patatas a la olla. Mezcla 1 CDA de maicena con agua en un vasito aparte y añadir a la olla hasta que la salsa espese. Apagar el fuego. Añadir 250g de guisantes congelados y sal al gusto. Remover y tapar. Los guisantes se cocinarán en 5 mins con el calor residual. Servir.

Sauté 2 chopped onions in olive oil with 1 tsp each sweet and spicy paprika. Add 4 sliced carrots. Add 50g chunky soya (TVP) and a pinch of salt. When the oil and spices are absorbed add 125ml red wine plus enough water to cover the ingredients. Simmer until carrots are cooked. Remove from the heat.

Separately cube 2 potatoes and deep fry in vegetable oil. When golden add them to the pan. In a cup mix 1 TBL of cornflour in a little water and add to the pan, cooking everything together until the mix thickens. Remove from the heat. Stir in 250g frozen peas and salt to taste. Cover to retain the heat. The peas will 'cook' within 5 mins and retain their colour. Serve.

tarta francesa   french onion tart

in HANDING IT ON there is a FRENCH QUICHE recipe, however it does not call for tofu

*Precalentar el horno a 130°C. Cocinar en una sartén, hasta que las cebollas estén MUY tiernas y caramelizadas, 4 **cebollas** en medias lunas, **aceite de oliva** (bastante cantidad), 1 cdt de **sal** y 1 CDA de **azúcar**. Una vez cocinadas separar las cebollas del aceite y guardar el aceite. Cubrir la base de un **molde redondo desmontable de silicona** de 1500ml con **sémola de maíz** y colocar la cebolla caramelizada sobre la sémola. Aparte preparar la masa. Batir 250g de **tofu duro**, 500ml de **leche de soja**, 100g de **maicena** y el aceite de las cebollas. Añadir sal al gusto. Echar la masa al molde. Espolvorear un poco de **pimienta negra** encima. Hornear durante 40 mins o hasta que la tartaleta esté firme.*

hay una receta para QUICHE FRANCESA en nuestro libro de platos salados, MANO a MANO... pero no lleva tofu...

Preheat the oven to 130°C. Sauté 4 onions cut in half moons in a good amount of olive oil with 1 tsp of salt and 1 TBL of sugar until the onions are VERY soft and caramelised. Remove the onions. Set aside oil. Ideally use a 1500ml round silicone ceramic-based springform mould and cover the base with polenta, then the caramelised onions. Whizz 250g tofu with 500ml soya milk, 100g cornflour & the olive oil from the onions. Salt to taste. Add to the mould. Sprinkle black pepper on the top and bake 40 mins or until the tart is set.

Mash up 10 cooked *potatoes* with *salt*, the juice of 1 *lemon*, a pinch of *turmeric* & ½ a whizzed *chilli*.

Separately, prepare a *filling* - mayo salad or guacamole or even leftovers...

Ideally use a *1500ml round silicone ceramic-based springform mould*. Cover the base with a layer of potato, then filling, then potato (it can be 5 layers if preferred). Top with *tofu mayo (p17)*. Garnish with chopped *red pepper* **and** *parsley*. Serve cold.

Cocer 10 **patatas** y usar para hacer un puré (con prensapatatas o tenedor). Aderezar con **sal**, el zumo de 1 **limón**, una pizca de **cúrcuma** y ½ **guindilla roja** triturada.

Aparte, preparar un **relleno** – como ensaladilla rusa o guacamole o usar sobras del frigorífico...
En un **molde redondo desmontable de silicona**, cubrir la base con una capa de puré de patata. Añadir el relleno y encima la otra capa de patata (también se puede hacer 3 capas de patata y 2 rellenos).

Echar por encima una **mayonesa de tofu** (p17).
Decorar con **pimiento rojo** picado y **perejil**. Dejar enfriar. Servir frío.

empanadas   pasties

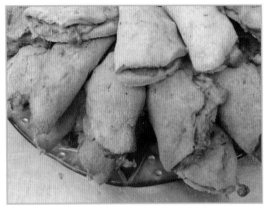

gluten-free pastry is the devil to make - here, step by step, are the tricks we have learned - the result is a melt-in-the-mouth delicious pastry that will not make you tear out your hair...

hacer masa sin gluten es todo un reto - aquí están los trucos que usamos en EL PIANO, paso por paso...

cold hands make better pastry	con las manos frías se hace la mejor masa
wet hands can prevent pastry sticking to them	la masa no se pega tanto a las manos mojadas
roll the dough out on a silicone baking sheet	estirar la masa sobre un salvabandejas de silicona
the more fat to flour the more melt-in-the-mouth factor, use from ¼-½ fat to flour	más grasa, más se funde en la boca. Usar desde ¼ hasta ½ de grasa por unidad de harina
try not to over-work the dough, roll it out quickly and evenly	intentar no manipular la masa demasiado y estirarla rápidamente
instead of turning the dough to roll it out, turn the silicone baking sheet around	en vez de girar la masa, girar el salvabandejas de silicona

Precalentar el horno a 170°C. Mezclar bien 125g de margarina con 250g de harina de sarraceno y una pizca de sal. Añadir agua fría para formar la masa.

1. Tener a mano un rodillo, una espátula y un salvabandejas de silicona.
2. Estirar la masa SOBRE el salvabandejas y cortar en círculos.
3. Colocar algún relleno en la mitad de cada círculo. Usar la espátula para doblar y cerrar las empanadas.
4. Deslizar el salvabandejas encima de la rejilla del horno.
5. Hornear a 150°C o hasta que estén crujientes.

Una opción es semi-hornearlas y congelar. Sacar del congelador 15 min antes y hornear 10 min.

Preheat oven to 170°C. Crumb 125g *margarine* with 250g *buckwheat flour* and a pinch of *salt*. Add cold *water* to make the pastry.

1. Have *rolling pin*, *spatula* & *silicone baking sheet* at hand.
2. Roll out pastry ON the silicone sheet & cut circles.
3. Put any filling on half the circle. Fold and close with the spatula.
4. Slide the silicone sheet onto the oven rack.
5. Bake at 150°C or until crispy.

Another option is semi-bake & freeze. Remove from freezer 15 min in advance & bake 10 mins.

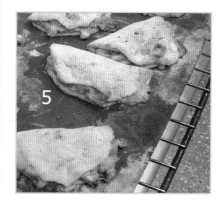

Plan, per person, on a handful of oyster mushrooms, 3 slices of fresh ginger, 1 chopped spring onion and 1 tsp of tamari.

Heat sunflower oil in a frying pan or on a griddle. Sauté everything EXCEPT the tamari. Cover with a silicone baking sheet. When the mushrooms are golden add the tamari and toss.

Ready!

Pensar en un puñado de setas, 3 láminas de jengibre, ½ cebolleta picada y 1 cdt de tamari por persona.

Calentar aceite de girasol en una sartén o a la plancha. Sofreír todo EXCEPTO el tamari y cubrir con un salvabandejas de silicona. Cuando las setas estén doradas añadir el tamari y remover.

¡Listas!

Tener a mano la hoja de algas nori, el arroz cocido y verduras de colores diferentes cortadas en tiras.
*Have to hand the **nori** sheets, cooked rice and different coloured **vegetables** cut in strips.*

Aplastar el arroz encima del nori.
Flatten the rice onto the nori.

Y ahora las verduras.
And now the vegetables.

Enrollar el nori.
Roll the nori.

Dejar resposar, la costura abajo.
Leave to rest, seam to the bottom.

Cortar en rodajas gruesas. Servir con tamari, jengibre y wasabi.
*Cut in cross sections. Serve with **tamari**, **ginger** & **wasabi**.*

tallarines noodles

Cook 250g of rice noodles *(or other type)*. Drain and set aside.

Chop 1 *red onion* in half moons and sauté in *sunflower* or *sesame oil* with a little fresh *ginger*. Slice julienne-style 2 *carrots*, ½ *red pepper*, ½ *green pepper* and ½ *courgette* and add to the pan.

Once the vegetables are cooked (crunchy if you prefer), add the noodles and a splash of *tamari*. Thicken the sauce with a little *cornflour* by mixing the cornflour separately in a glass with water. As a final touch, sprinkle chopped *spring onions* over the top.

Cocinar 250g de tallarines de arroz (u otra variedad). Escurrir.

Aparte, sofreír 1 cebolla roja cortada en medias lunas en aceite de girasol o sésamo. Añadir un poco de jengibre fresco, 2 zanahorias, ½ pimiento rojo, 1 pimiento verde largo y ½ calabacín, todo cortado en tiras finas.

Una vez hechas las verduras (crujientes si las prefiere así), añadir los tallarines y aderezar con tamari al gusto. Espesar la salsa con un poco de maicena (mezclada con agua en un vaso aparte). Como toque final, picar tallos verdes de cebolleta y decorar por encima.

no cholesterol citrus 'cheese'cake
tarta de 'queso' sin colesterol

sugarless apple cake
pastel de manzana sin azúcar

brownie with beet colouring
colorante remolacha

When we began devising our recipes in 1997 all we had to guide us was an already arduous career in vegetarian wholefood baking. Although it was a leap to remove all the animal products and all the gluten (which does not leave the vegetarian wholefood baker much to work with), we did at least understand HOW stuff works...

YEAST *is live. Salt kills it. It needs sugar to feed it and warmth to multiply and thereby lift the dough*
BAKING POWDER *is activated by moisture and heat*
BAKING SODA *is also activated by moisture and heat but acts faster Whether baking powder or soda, the minute the cake is mixed, in the oven with it!*

Taking these recipes as a base you should be able to adapt them for your own preferences...

Cuando empezamos a crear nuestras recetas en 1997, nuestra experiencia anterior había sido en la panadería integral y vegetariana. Aunque fue un gran reto quitar todos los productos animales y todo el gluten (que en realidad no deja muchos ingredientes para un panadero de pan integral y vegetariano), por lo menos entendíamos CÓMO funcionan los ingredientes...

La LEVADURA MADRE está viva. La sal la mata. Necesita alimentarse con azúcar y estar calentita para multiplicarse y doblar la masa
La LEVADURA EN POLVO se activa con humedad y calor
El BICARBONATO DE SODIO también se activa con humedad y calor pero es menos estable
En ambos casos, una vez que la masa esté mezclada, hay que meterla en el horno rápido.

Nuestras recetas deben darle una base para adaptarlas a su gusto...

61

flours harinas

Harina puede ser casi cualquier alimento molido hasta conseguir un polvo fino.

Normalmente se trata de trigo, cebada, centeno... Pero, una vez que empecemos a ver cualquier alimento como posible harina, empieza la diversión....

Harina de garbanzos - garbanzos molidos
Papadums de la India se hacen con lentejas molidas
Cacao - los granos molidos
Mostaza - las semillas molidas
Harina de arroz se puede hacer en casa con un molino de café usando el arroz en grano
Harina de maíz - los granos de maíz molidos y maicena es la versión más refinada
Harina de sarraceno no es un cereal molido. Son semillas molidas de una planta herbácea, y por eso es apta para celiacos
Café - los granos molidos
Pimentón - pimientos molidos
Harina de patatas - secas y molidas

Ahora podemos empezar a experimentar. Por ejemplo, podemos usar cacao para salsas dulces, mostaza o pimentón dulce para salsa bechamel...o para la base de cremas o de un CHOWDER (p26)...

Flour is virtually anything that is milled to a powder.

Typically this is wheat, barley, rye... But once we begin to the see ANYTHING that is milled as a flour, the fun begins...

Gram flour - milled chickpeas
Papadums - made from milled lentils
Cocoa - milled cocoa beans
Mustard - milled mustard seeds
Rice flour - milled rice (which, if you find yourself without, can be milled in a coffee grinder from whole rice)
Polenta/cornmeal/maize flour - coarsely milled corn kernels and cornflour - the highly refined version
Buckwheat flour is not from milled grain but is the milled seeds of a herbaceous plant, hence its ready use for people with coeliac disease
Coffee - milled beans
Paprika - milled peppers
Potato flour - dried and milled

Now we can start to experiment with flours using, for example, cocoa for sweet sauces, or mustard or sweet paprika to make bechamel... or a soup or CHOWDER base (p26)...

pastel de manzana apple cake

sin azúcar añadido
without added sugar

This can easily be made with pears, plums, blackberries or indeed any fruit that is naturally sweet

En vez de manzanas se puede usar cualquier otra fruta dulce como peras, ciruelas, moras...

Pre-heat the oven to 150°C. Grate 12 eating apples into a bowl. Add 200g margarine and 1 tsp pure vanilla. Beat in 600ml any fruit juice, 350g buckwheat flour, 100g raisins (optional), 25g baking powder and a pinch of salt. Spoon into a 1500ml silicone mould. Decorate the top with sliced apples. Bake 150°C 50-60 mins until the cake is solid. Cool, cut and serve.

*Precalentar el horno a 150°C. Rallar 12 **manzanas** dulces. Añadir 200g de **margarina** y 1 cdt de **vainilla pura**. Mezclar con 600ml de **zumo** de cualquier fruta, 350g de **harina de sarraceno**, 100g de **pasas** (opcional), 25g de **levadura** y una pizca de **sal**. Echar todo en un **molde de silicona** de 1500ml. Adornar por encima con rodajas de manzana. Hornear 50-60 mins hasta que el pastel esté firme. Dejar enfriar, cortar y servir.*

pastel de plátanos banana cake

a fantastic cake for reducing sugar - we then offer the option of icing and chocolate for those who love it sweeter

un pastel fantástico si quiere reducir el consumo de azúcar - existe la opción de servirlo con glaseado y chocolate

Precalentar el horno a
Preheat oven to
150°C

Batir 5 plátanos con 250g de margarina. Añadir 600ml de zumo de cualquier fruta, 25g de levadura, 400g de harina de sarraceno y una pizca de sal. Echar en un molde de silicona de 1500ml y hornear 45 mins hasta que cuando se meta un cuchillo salga limpio. Dejar que se enfríe.

El glaseado es plátanos batidos con azúcar glacé.

Whizz 5 bananas with 250g of margarine. When well blended add 600ml fruit juice, 25g of baking powder, 400g buckwheat flour and a pinch of salt. Pour into a 1500ml silicone mould. Bake 45 mins until a knife when slid into the centre comes away clean. Leave to cool.

The icing is bananas beaten with icing sugar.

sin azúcar añadido
without added sugar

este pastel es, sin duda, el MÁS caro de todos los pasteles que hacemos
SIN EMBARGO la quinoa tiene muchos beneficios nutritivos y ésta es una forma excelente de incluirla en nuestra dieta

Precalentar el horno a 150°C. En una olla derretir 250g de margarina con 500ml de sirope de fruta como SWEET FREEDOM, 50g de jengibre rallado y una pizca de sal. Una vez hervido quitar del fuego y añadir 500g de copos de quinoa, 150g de harina de maíz y 25g de levadura. Hornear 10-15 mins en un molde de silicona de 1500ml. Dejar en el molde y cortar antes de que se enfríe. ¡Cuidado de no cortar el molde!

Preheat the oven to 150°C. Melt 250g margarine in a pan with 500ml fruit syrup (SWEET FREEDOM), 50g grated fresh ginger and a pinch of salt. Once boiled, remove from heat & add 500g quinoa flakes, 150g maize flour & 25g baking powder. Bake 10-15 min in a square 1500ml silicone mould. Leave in the mould & cut before cool. Take care not to cut the silicone!

this is without doubt the MOST expensive dessert we have ever made...HOWEVER, quinoa is an extremely beneficial ingredient and this is an excellent way to include it in your diet

compôte

se puede conservar en tarros como chutney (p15)

can be preserved in pickling jars (p15)

Choose a variety of seasonal fruits, calculate 3 fruits per person. In the autumn, fruit such as pears, plums, apples, in the summer, fruit such as peaches, strawberries, raspberries, grapes. Slice, removing any stones, but do not peel. Simmer lightly in little water until soft. Chill and serve.

*Elegir una variedad de **fruta de temporada**. Calcular 3 frutas por persona. En otoño elegir frutas como peras, ciruelas, manzanas. En verano elegir melocotones, fresas, frambuesas, uvas. Cortar en trozos y quitar los huesos sin pelar. Cocinar en poca **agua** a fuego lento hasta que las frutas estén blandas. Enfriar y servir.*

pastel de tahin   tahini raisin loaf

sin azúcar añadido
without added sugar

a semi-sweet nutty loaf, this can be eaten as dessert or to accompany savoury dishes

medio dulce, se puede comer este pan como pastel o para acompañar platos salados

Pre-heat the oven to 150°C. Grate 2 courgettes into a bowl. Add 50ml olive oil, 250ml tahini, 500ml rice milk, 1 tsp cinnamon, 1 tsp pure vanilla, 200g raisins, 500g buckwheat flour, 25g baking powder and a pinch of salt. Turn into 2 1000ml silicone loaf pans. Bake 150°C 90 mins until the cake is solid. Cool, cut and serve.

Precalentar el horno a 150°C. Rallar 2 **calabacines**. Añadir 50ml de **aceite de oliva**, 250ml de **tahin** (crema de sésamo), 500ml de **leche de arroz**, 1 cdt de **canela**, 1 cdt de **vainilla pura**, 200g de **pasas**, 500g de **harina de sarraceno**, 25g de **levadura** y una pizca de **sal**. Meter todo en 2 **moldes de silicona** de 1000ml. Hornear 90 mins hasta que los pasteles estén firmes. Dejar enfriar, cortar y servir.

67

pastel luna moon cake

> *essentially this is layers of batter between layers of fresh fruit - no sugar, no soya and low in fat* - este pastel es capas de masa con capas de fruta fresca - nada de azúcar - nada de soja - bajo en grasa

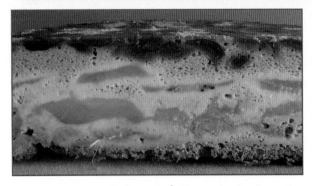

Precalentar el horno a 150°C

Preheat oven to 150°C

Cortar en rodajas 4 ó 5 variedades de fruta fresca: plátanos, kiwi, mango, naranja... Dejar aparte.

Cut 4 or 5 types of fresh fruit into strips: bananas, oranges, mango, kiwi... Set aside.

Batir la masa: 200ml de aceite de girasol, 350g de harina de sarraceno, 1 CDA de levadura, 600ml de cualquier zumo y una pizca de sal. En un molde de silicona de 1500ml, alternar capas de fruta y masa empezando con fruta y terminando con masa. Meter en el horno 1 hora y después bajar a 100°C 1 hora más.

Whizz the batter: 200ml sunflower oil, 350g buckwheat flour, 1 TBL baking powder, 600ml any fruit juice and a pinch of salt. Alternate layers of fresh fruit with batter in a 1500ml silicone mould, start with a fruit layer, end with batter. Bake 1 hour. Lower the temperature to 100°C and bake 1 more hour.

Dejar que se enfríe. Darle la vuelta antes de cortar. La fruta está por encima.

Cool & turn before cutting. Fruit then shows on the top.

pastel de dátiles   sticky toffee pudding

el pastel no lleva azúcar añadido - la salsa ¡SÍ!
the cake has no added sugar - the sauce does!

el pastel CON la salsa se llama STICKY TOFFEE PUDDING y tiene mucha fama en Inglaterra...
WITH sauce this is the well-known British STICKY TOFFEE PUDDING

Preheat oven to 150°C. Heat 500g margarine with 500g dried dates. Whizz. Add 350g chickpea flour (gram/garbanzo bean flour), 1L soya milk, 5ml pure vanilla, a pinch of salt and 25g baking powder. Whizz. Pour into a 1500ml silicone mould. Bake 30-40 mins.

*Precalentar el horno a 150°C. Calentar 500g de **margarina** con 500g de **dátiles**. Batir y añadir 350g de **harina de garbanzos**, 1L de **leche de soja**, 5ml de **vainilla pura**, una pizca de **sal** y 25g de **levadura**. Batir. Verter en un **molde de silicona** de 1500ml. Hornear 30-40 mins.*

DOS opciones de cobertura - TWO topping options
la de la foto es simplemente dátiles batidos con un poco de agua -
la salsa para STICKY TOFFEE PUDDING es 1 unidad de margarina derretida
con 2 unidades de azúcar moreno, una pizca de sal y vainilla pura al gusto
the topping in the photo is simply dates whizzed with water -
STICKY TOFFEE PUDDING sauce is 1 unit of margarine melted with 2 units of brown sugar, a pinch of salt and pure vanilla to taste

tassajara

El Piano's homage to the cuisine of Tassajara... a raw fruit dessert inspired by Tassajara Bread Book

homenaje de El Piano a la cocina de Tassajara... un postre crudo de frutas inspirado por el libro Tassajara Bread Book

Invest in baking rings or simply use a small short tin can with the top and bottom removed. Squashed bananas and soaked, then whizzed dried dates or apricots are the 'glues'. Put the ring into the muffin paper. Alternately layer in seasonal fresh fruit and the 'glues'. Decorate the top. Slide off the ring.

*Comprar **anillos** o simplemente usar una lata pequeña y baja sin la tapa y sin la base. Hacer 'pegamentos' usando **plátanos** aplastados y **orejones** o **dátiles** remojados y batidos. Colocar el anillo en un **molde de magdalena**. Alternar capas de los 'pegamentos' con **frutas frescas de temporada**. Adornar y quitar el anillo.*

they will not last more than 8 hours
no duran más de 8 horas

pacific poké

sin azúcar añadido, sin sal añadida y sin grasa añadida
without added salt, fat or sugar

una receta de Indonesia... esta tarta es sencilla, con un sabor delicado - servir fría o caliente

originally from Indonesia, this recipe yields a simple-to-make tart with a delicate flavour to serve hot or cold

Pre-heat the oven to 150°C. Cover the base of a 1500ml springform silicone mould with a shallow layer of cornmeal/polenta. Break 12 bananas into a bowl. Add 200g block of creamed coconut and a pinch of cinnamon. Add warm water to just cover the contents of the bowl. Whizz. Pour into the mould over the cornmeal. Bake 150°C 20-30 mins until the pie is solid.

Precalentar el horno a 150°C. Cubrir la base de un **molde desmontable de silicona** de 1500ml con una capa muy fina de **sémola de maíz**. Echar 12 **plátanos** en un bol con 200g bloque de **crema de coco** y una pizca de **canela**. Añadir suficiente **agua** caliente para cubrir casi todos los ingredientes. Batir. Verter en el molde y hornear 20-30 mins hasta que la tarta esté firme.

anillo de arroz   rice ring

Hervir 1L de leche de arroz. Añadir 250g de arroz, 250g de pasas, 12 cardamomos verdes, la piel de 1 limón, 5ml de vainilla pura y una pizca de sal. Tapar y bajar el fuego. Cocinar 20 mins. Mientras, mezclar bien 150ml de agua con 250g de harina de arroz. Añadir a la olla y seguir cocinando, removiendo constantemente. Cuando la mezcla hierva quitar del fuego y echar en un molde de silicona de 1L en forma de anillo. Enfriar 24 horas. Desmoldar, cortar y servir. 8 trozos.

Boil 1L of rice milk. Add 250g of rice, 250g of raisins, 12 green cardamoms, the peel of 1 lemon, 5ml pure vanilla and a pinch of salt. Cover. Reduce heat & cook 20 mins. In a cup mix 150ml water and 250g of rice flour to a smooth paste. Add to the pan. Continue cooking, stirring constantly. When the mix boils remove from the heat and spoon into a 1L silicone ring mould. Cool 24 hours, turn out, cut. Serves 8.

no fat
no added sugar
no soya

sin grasa
sin azúcar
añadido
sin soja

pastel de albaricoque   apricot cake

sin azúcar añadido
no added sugar

el pastel de la foto es sin cobertura - se puede hacer una cobertura sin azúcar añadido - batir orejones remojados con un poco de agua, nada más...

the cake pictured has no topping - it's easy to make a sugar-free topping - whizz soaked dried apricots with water, nothing more...

Preheat the oven to 150°C. Cover 750g dried apricots with soya milk and heat with 125g margarine. Whizz. Add 150g chickpea flour (gram/garbanzo bean flour), 25ml pure vanilla, 35g baking powder and any additional soya milk necessary for a cake consistency. Whizz. Pour into a 1500ml silicone mould. Bake 150°C 30-40 mins.

Precalentar el horno a 150°C. Cubrir 750g de **orejones** con **leche de soja**. Calentar con 125g de **margarina**. Batir. Añadir 150g de **harina de garbanzos**, 25ml de **vainilla pura**, 35g de **levadura** y leche adicional si es necesario para conseguir la consistencia de un pastel. Batir y verter en un **molde de silicona** de 1500ml. Hornear 30-40 mins.

73

pastel de boda   bridal slice

Bridal slice is an old bakery trick for using up stale cakes. At EL PIANO GRANADA the climate, combined with refrigeration, dries cakes out very quickly. We use the technique to moisten **dry cakes***. Break up the cakes in a bowl. Add* **rice milk, soya milk** *or* **fruit juice** *and whizz adding more liquid until it has a cake consistency. Add 50g* **baking powder** *per 1500ml of mix. Turn into* **silicone moulds***. Bake 45 mins at 150°C. Decorate to taste.*

Este pastel es un truco de panadero para gastar pasteles secos. En EL PIANO GRANADA, con el clima y la refrigeración, los pasteles pueden secarse rápido. Usamos la técnica para mojarlos. Romper los **pasteles** en un bol con **leche de soja, leche de arroz** o **zumo** y batir hasta que la masa tenga la consistencia de una masa de pastel. Añadir 50g de **levadura** por cada 1500ml. Verter en **moldes de silicona** y hornear 45 mins a 150°C. Adornar a su gusto.

without added fat
sin grasa añadida

an exquisite and easy to make dessert - the glass serving dishes give it a special touch

un postre exquisito que es también muy fácil de hacer - las copas le dan un toque muy especial

Leave 250g of any summer fruit in sugar overnight. The quantity of sugar is entirely at your discretion. The sugar will draw out the juices of the fruit. Measure the result, and, if necessary, remove some, or add water, so that the level is 500ml. Heat. Mix 1 TBL cornflour in 200ml soya milk or rice milk. Add to the heated fruit pulp. Stir constantly as it thickens. As soon as it boils, remove, whizz and turn into 4 glass dishes. Refrigerate. Garnish and serve.

Dejar 250g de cualquier **fruta de verano** en **azúcar** la noche antes. La cantidad de azúcar es a su gusto. El azúcar hará que salga el jugo de la fruta. Medir la mezcla, y, si es necesario, quitar algo, o añadir **agua**, hasta que mida 500ml. Calentar. Mezclar 1 CDA de **maicena** con 200ml de **leche de soja** o **leche de arroz**. Añadirlo a la fruta removiendo constantemente. Cuando hierva, quitar del fuego, batir y dividir entre 4 **copas**. Dejar que se enfríe, adornar y servir.

tartas/pies: chocolate

ambas tartas tienen una base de pasta horneada - el relleno se hace aparte y se echa antes de enfriar - se puede variar la receta simplemente cambiando el sabor del relleno

both tarts have a pre-cooked pastry shell - the filling is cooked separately and poured into the pie shell before cooling - the recipe can be varied simply by changing the flavours of the filling

Preparar la base. La receta es la misma que se usa para las empanadas (p57). Usar un **molde de silicona** y hornear hasta que esté crujiente.

Prepare the pastry case. The recipe is the same as for the pasties (p57). Use a silicone mould and bake until crisp.

Mix and heat	Mezclar y calentar
1150ml rice milk	1150ml leche arroz
250ml sugar	250g azúcar
75g cocoa powder	75g cacao
200g rice flour	200g harina arroz
1 TBL cornflour	1 CDA maicena
25ml pure vanilla	25ml vainilla pura
pinch of salt	pizca de sal
Stir constantly until it boils. Pour over the base and leave to cool 24 hours.	Cocinar y remover constantemente hasta que hierva. Verter encima de la base y enfriar 24 horas.

tartas/pies: limón/lemon

Mix and heat	Mezclar y calentar
1150ml **soya milk**	1150ml *leche soja*
250g **sugar**	250g *azúcar*
3 **lemons**, (juice & grated peel)	3 *limones (zumo y ralladura)*
1 TBL **margarine**	1 CDA *margarina*
4 TBL **cornflour**	4 CDA *maicena*
pinch of **salt**	*pizca de sal*
pinch of **turmeric**	*pizca de cúrcuma*

Stir constantly until it boils. Pour over the base and leave to cool 24 hours.

Cocinar y remover constantemente hasta que hierva. Verter encima de la base y enfriar 24 horas.

EL TOQUE FINAL...   THE FINAL TOUCH...
cubrir la tarta de chocolate con queso de soja mezclado con azúcar y decorar con chocolate rallado - decorar la de limón con ralladura
cover the chocolate pie with soya cheese mixed with sugar and with grated chocolate - sprinkle lemon peel on the lemon pie

brownie, traditional & andalusian

Preheat oven to 170°C. Melt 250g margarine in a bowl, add	Precalentar el horno a 170°C. Derretir 250g de margarina en una fuente. Añadir

Preheat oven to 170°C. Melt 250g margarine in a bowl, add

- *250g brown sugar*
- *500ml soya milk*
- *300g buckwheat flour*
- *75g pure cocoa*
- *5ml pure vanilla*
- *25g baking powder*
- *pinch of salt*

Whizz and bake 5 mins in 1500ml mould (or equivalent) at 170°C. Reduce heat to 130°C for 40 mins.
Cool, turn out & eat!

Precalentar el horno a 170°C. Derretir 250g de margarina en una fuente. Añadir

- 250g azúcar moreno
- 500ml leche de soja
- 300g harina de sarraceno
- 75g cacao puro
- 5ml vainilla pura
- 25g levadura
- pizca de sal

Batir. Hornear en un molde de 1500ml (o equivalente) durante 5 mins a 170°C. Reducir a 130°C 40 mins más. Sacar, dejar enfriar y ¡a comer!

This is not a traditional cake mix needing care so that eggs and milk do not curdle. Just mix all together, sling it in the oven and presto, pretty well perfect every time. For the Andalus version use rice milk instead of soya and habas/fava bean/broad bean flour instead of buckwheat. Another variation is to substitute sunflower oil for the margarine and orange juice for the milk. It will take any shape!

Éste no es un bizcocho tradicional, no hay que tener cuidado con los huevos y que la leche que no se corte. Simplemente mezclarlo todo, meter en el horno, y, voilà, perfecto... Para la version Andaluza, usar leche de arroz en vez de soja, y harina de habas en vez de harina de sarraceno. Otra versión es sustituir aceite de girasol por la margarina y zumo de naranja por la leche. ¡Siempre sale bien!

gulab jaman

Hacer el sirope. Hervir 300ml de agua con 600ml (volumen) de azúcar, mitad moreno/mitad blanco, 12 cardamomos verdes y 3 ramas de canela. Quitar del fuego, añadir agua de rosa al gusto y dejar aparte.

*Hacer la masa. Mezclar 2L (volumen) de mijo cocido con 125ml (volumen) de harina de sarraceno, 30g de levadura, la ralladura de 1 limón y 1 naranja y 125ml de agua. Formar bolitas **sin apretar** y freír en abundante aceite vegetal hasta que estén doradas. Quitar del aceite y sumergir en el sirope caliente. Dejar que se enfríen FUERA del frigorífico.*

Make a syrup by boiling 300ml water with 600ml (by volume) sugar, half brown/half white, 12 green cardamoms and 3 cinnamon sticks. Remove from heat. Add rose water to taste. Set aside.

Mix a dough of 2L (by volume) cooked millet with 125ml (by volume) buckwheat flour, 30g baking powder, grated peel of 1 orange and 1 lemon and 125ml water. Form balls but **don't press them together hard**. Deep fry until golden. Submerge in the warm syrup. Cool OUTSIDE of the fridge.

Syrup soaked balls of heaven, gulab jaman are an Asian dessert made of milk powder and wheat flour...our version has taken years to develop to get the same texture and taste explosion...

Bañadas en sirope, estas bolitas son divinas. Un dulce de la India, la receta tradicional lleva lactosa y trigo - nos ha costado años de trabajo para desarrollar la nuestra y ahora puede experimentar la ¡explosión de sabor!

lemon & ginger cake   pastel de jengibre y limón

Preheat oven to 170°C.
Melt 250g margarine in a bowl. Add

- *250g brown sugar*
- *500ml soya milk*
- *350g buckwheat flour*
- *100g fresh grated ginger*
- *juice of 3 lemons*
- *5ml pure vanilla*
- *25g baking powder*
- *pinch of salt*

Whizz. Bake 5 mins in 1500ml mould (or equivalent). Reduce heat to 130°C for 40 more minutes.
Cool, turn out & eat!

Precalentar el horno a 170°C. Derretir 250g de margarina en una fuente. Añadir

- 250g azúcar moreno
- 500ml leche de soja
- 350g harina de sarraceno
- 100g jengibre fresco rallado
- zumo de 3 limones
- 5ml vainilla pura
- 25g levadura
- pizca de sal

Batir. Hornear en un molde de 1500ml (o equivalente) 5 mins. Reducir a 130°C para 40 mins más. Sacar, dejar enfriar y ¡a comer!

The topping is particularly delicious, tart yet sweet. Mix approx. 300g icing sugar with the juice of 1 lemon. Apply half of it while the cake is hot so it soaks in, and the other half when the cake is cold, just before serving.

El glaseado es especialmente delicioso, dulce pero también ácido. Mezclar aprox. 300g de azúcar glacé con el zumo de 1 limón. Untar la mitad encima del pastel cuando esté todavía calentito para que 'chupe' el glaseado y la otra mitad cuando el pastel esté frío.

marble cake pastel de mármol

precalentar el horno a 170°C - preparar 2 masas separadas - asegurar de tener todo preparado antes de echar la levadura

preheat the oven to 170°C - prepare 2 mixes separately - make sure you have everything ready before adding the baking powder

Masa 1

Derretir 125g de margarina en una fuente. Añadir

- 125g azúcar moreno
- 250ml leche de soja
- 150g harina de sarraceno
- 35g cacao puro
- 5ml vainilla pura
- 25g levadura
- pizca de sal

Masa 2

Derretir 125g de margarina en una fuente. Añadir

- 125g azúcar moreno
- 250ml zumo de naranja
- 175g harina de sarraceno
- 5ml vainilla pura
- 25g levadura
- pizca de sal

Batir cada masa. Echar las masas en capas en un molde de 1500ml (o equivalente) y remover para crear el efecto de mármol. Hornear durante 5 mins a 170°C. Reducir a 130°C 40 mins más. Sacar, dejar enfriar y ia comer!

Mix 1
Melt 125g margarine in a bowl, add

- *125g brown sugar*
- *250ml soya milk*
- *150g buckwheat flour*
- *35g pure cocoa*
- *5ml pure vanilla*
- *25g baking powder*
- *pinch of salt*

Mix 2
Melt 125g margarine in a bowl, add

- *125g brown sugar*
- *250ml orange juice*
- *175g buckwheat flour*
- *5ml pure vanilla*
- *25g baking powder*
- *pinch of salt*

Whizz each mix. Pour the mixes in layers into a 1500ml mould (or equivalent) and stir to create a marble effect. Bake 5 mins at 170°C. Reduce heat to 130°C for 40 mins. Cool, turn out & eat!

81

carrot cake   pastel de zanahoria

el glaseado se encuentra en p13

you can find the icing on p13

precalentar el horno a 170°C

preheat oven to 170°C

Put 4 handfuls of **grated carrots** in a bowl. Add	*Meter 4 puñados de zanahorias ralladas en una fuente. Añadir*
250g **brown sugar** 250ml **sunflower oil** 1 **orange**, juice & grated peel 500g **buckwheat flour** 100g **raisins** 15g ground **cinnamon** 5ml pure **vanilla** 25g **baking powder** a pinch of **salt**	*250g azúcar moreno* *250ml aceite de girasol* *1 naranja, zumo y ralladura* *500g harina de sarraceno* *100g pasas* *15g canela molida* *5ml vainilla pura* *25g levadura* *pizca de sal*
Mix thoroughly by hand. Bake in **1500ml** mould (or equivalent) 15 mins. Reduce to 130°C for 60 more minutes. Cool, turn out & eat!	*Mezclar bien a mano. Hornear en un molde de 1500ml (o equivalente) 15 mins. Reducir a 130°C para 60 min más. Sacar, dejar enfriar y ¡a comer!*

florida lime pie   tarta de lima de florida

cook millet 20 mins - 1 unit of grain to 2.5 units of water... any left over use as cous cous

cocinar mijo 20 mins - 1 unidad de mijo por 2,5 unidades de agua... si sobra usarlo para hacer cuscús

Cook together 100g margarine, 400g cooked millet, 100g sugar and 5ml pure vanilla. When golden brown remove and cover the bottom of a 1500ml silicone springform mould. Put grated peel & juice of 8 limes in a 1500ml jug. Add 200g sugar, 180g cornflour and a pinch of salt. Top up with water. Cook slowly stirring constantly. When mix thickens fully pour into the mould. Cover and leave to chill 24 hours.

Cocinar juntos 100g de margarina, 400g de mijo cocido, 100g de azúcar y 5ml de vainilla pura. Cuando esté dorado quitar del fuego y usar para cubrir el fondo de un molde desmontable de silicona de 1500ml. Poner la ralladura y el zumo de 8 limas en una jarra de 1500ml. Añadir 200g de azúcar, 180g de maicena y una pizca de sal. Añadir agua hasta 1500ml. Cocinar la mezcla lentamente removiendo constantemente. Cuando espese del todo, verter en el molde. Cubrir y dejar enfriar 24 horas.

83

'cheese'cake 1   tarta de 'queso' 1

ambas tartas tienen una base de sémola de maíz y están basadas en soja; leche de soja o tofu - nuestra versión clásica es con frutas cítricas, pero se puede cambiar el sabor y color añadiendo frutas del bosque

both cheesecakes have a polenta base and both use soya, if not soya milk then tofu - our classic version is citrus, but it is simple to whizz in summer fruits and change the flavour and the colour

Preheat the oven to 130°C. Cover the base of a 1500ml silicone springform mould with a fine sprinkling of polenta. Grate the peel of 1 lemon, 1 lime and 1 orange and set aside. Prepare the filling. Whizz 250g tofu with 500ml soya milk, 1 tsp pure vanilla, 100g cornflour and the juice of the citric fruits. Add salt and sugar to taste. Pour the mix into the mould. Sprinkle the grated peel on top. Bake 50 mins or until firm.

Precalentar el horno a 130°C. Cubrir la base de un molde desmontable de silicona de 1500ml con una capa fina de sémola de maíz. Aparte, rallar la piel de 1 limón, 1 lima y 1 naranja. Preparar la masa. Batir 250g de tofu duro, 500ml de leche de soja, 1 cdt de vainilla pura, 100g de maicena y el zumo de las frutas cítricas. Añadir sal y azúcar al gusto. Echar la masa al molde. Espolvorear la ralladura encima. Hornear durante 50 mins o hasta que la tarta esté firme.

this version is cooked on the stove - both versions are virtually fat free and can be made in individual servings

esta versión se hace en la hornilla - ambas son practicamente totalmente sin grasa y se pueden hacer en cazuelas individuales

Cubrir la base de un **molde desmontable de silicona** de 1500ml con una capa fina de **sémola de maíz**. Preparar la masa. En una olla batir 1500ml de **leche de soja**, 350g de **azúcar** (con azúcar blanco sale una tarta pálida, con azúcar moreno sale más oscura), 1 cdt de **vainilla pura**, la ralladura y zumo de 5 **limones**, 250g de **maicena** y **sal** al gusto. Cocinar y remover constantemente hasta que espese. Verter encima de la sémola de maíz. Dejar enfriar 24 horas.

Cover the base of a 1500ml silicone springform mould with a fine sprinkling of polenta.
Prepare the filling in a pan whizzing 1500ml of soya milk with 350g sugar (using white sugar retains the pale colour, use brown and the colour darkens), 1 tsp pure vanilla, the grated peel and juice of 5 lemons, 250g of cornflour and a pinch of salt. Cook stirring constantly until the filling thickens. Pour onto the polenta. Cool overnight.

as with our savoury fritters, just about any fruit & spice can be used in this dish - to avoid sugar, dust with grated coconut

igual que las frituras saladas, se puede usar cualquier mezcla de fruta y especias para este plato - para evitar azúcar espolvorear con coco rallado

Chop a selection of festive dried fruits such as raisins, cherries, sultanas, apricots and dates. Cover with fresh orange and lemon juice and leave to soak overnight. Add exotic spices such as cinnamon, mace & cloves. Add rice flour to make a dough & a touch of brandy. Form into balls and deep fry in vegetable oil. Dust with icing sugar.

Picar una selección de frutas secas como pasas, cerezas, orejones de albaricoques y dátiles. Cubrir con zumo de naranjas y limones y dejar en remojo 24 horas. Añadir especias exóticas como canela, macis y clavo. Añadir harina de arroz para crear una masa y un toque de coñac. Formar bolitas y freír en abundante aceite vegetal. Espolvorear azúcar glacé encima.

RECETA UNIVERSAL RECIPE
Preheat oven/*precalentar el horno a* 150°C

Batir 250g de margarina con 250g de azúcar. Añadir 500ml de líquido; zumo o leche. Añadir 350g de harina de sarraceno, 25ml de vainilla pura y 25g de levadura. Verter en moldes de magdalena de silicona o papel. Hornear 15-20 mins.

Beat 250g margarine with 250g sugar. Add 500ml of liquid; juice or milk. Add 350g of buckwheat flour, 25ml of pure vanilla and 25g of baking powder. Pour into silicone or paper muffin moulds. Bake 15-20 mins.

for chocolate or coffee flavour replace 30g of the buckwheat flour with cocoa or instant coffee - try adding chocolate chips, raisins, cinnamon, chunks of fresh apple, keep experimenting...
para magdalenas de choco o café sustituir 30g de la harina por 30g de cacao o café. Experimentar con canela, pepitas de choco, manzana, pasas etc...

fast fudge & mint creams
dulces cremosos de chocolate y de hierbabuena

Batir 8 hojas grandes de hierbabuena con 2 CDA de agua. Mezclar bien con 1L (volumen) de azúcar glacé y una pizca de sal. Dejar en bolitas aplastadas encima de un salvabandejas de silicona hasta que se sequen.

Whizz 8 big mint leaves with 2 TBL of water. Mix well with 1L (by volume) of icing sugar. Leave the mix pressed into circles to dry on a silicone sheet.

Mezclar bien 1 unidad de margarina, 4 unidades de azúcar glacé y 1 unidad de cacao. Añadir zumo de limón, vainilla pura y sal al gusto. Prensar en un molde cuadrado para hacer cuadraditos o formar bolitas. Guardar en frío.

Mix well 1 unit of margarine with 4 units of icing sugar and 1 unit of cocoa. Add lemon juice, pure vanilla and salt to taste. Press into a square dish for squares or roll into balls. Refrigerate.

granada chai

a great favourite with many customers in Spain and the UK alike, the syrup is based on Arabic flavours and will last months in the fridge

muy popular tanto en España como en Inglaterra, este sirope está basado en sabores árabes y dura meses en el frigorífico

Hacer un sirope.
*Cocinar al fuego lento 500ml de **agua**, 2-3 bolsitas de **té negro**, ½ rama de **canela**, ½ cdt de **nuez moscada**, 10 **cardamomos verdes**, ½ **guindilla roja** picada, una pizca de **cilantro en grano** y **azúcar** al gusto.*

*Para hacer el chai, añadir el sirope al gusto a **leche** caliente.*

Make a syrup.
Simmer gently 500ml of water with 2-3 regular tea bags, ½ stick of cinnamon, ½ tsp nutmeg, 10 green cardamoms, ½ chopped red chilli, a pinch of coriander seeds and sugar to taste.

To make the chai, add syrup to taste to hot milk.

equipment & abbreviations

We talk about silicone moulds ALL THE TIME. Silicone is a variant of glass and similarly is made of sand (silica). Invest in them. Make sure they are 100% silicone and not laminated. NOTHING sticks to them, they are easy to clean and the results are perfect every time.

Whizz, refers to a stick blender which is indispensible in our line of work.

If you can only have one pan, choose a non-stick, deep, heavy and yes, expensive, frying pan with a lid. It can be used as a griddle, as a frying pan, and as a saucepan.

In MANO a MANO we measure most everything in terms of 500g margarine containers. THE FINAL TOUCH reverts to the more traditional use of grams and litres.

If you prefer the margarine tub method, a 500g margarine tub of buckwheat flour is around 350g and so on. You will need to do your own conversions.

TABLESPOON, around 50ml, is abbreviated to TBL and teaspoon, around 5ml, is abbreviated to tsp. Minutes are abbreviated to mins.

batería y abreviaciones

Mencionamos moldes de silicona por todo el libro. La silicona, como el vidrio, deriva de la arena (silicio). Vale la pena invertir en estos moldes. Asegurar que sean 100% silicona y no laminados. Nada se pega, son fáciles de limpiar y todo siempre sale perfecto.

Batir, se refiere a una batidora de mano que es imprescindible en esta cocina.

Si solo se puede tener un recipiente para cocinar, elegir una sartén antiadherente profunda y pesada, con tapa, y sí, cara. Puede usarla como plancha, sartén y, también, olla.

En *MANO a MANO* medimos casi todos los ingredientes usando el volumen de un envase de plástico de margarina de 500g. En *EL TOQUE FINAL* hemos vuelto al uso tradicional de gramos y litros. Si prefiere el método de volumen, un envase de margarina de 500g de harina de sarraceno pesa alrededor de 350g. Tendrá que hacer sus propias conversiones.

Una CUCHARADA, aprox. 50ml, se escribe CDA y una cucharadita, aprox. 5ml, se escribe cdt. La abreviación de minutos es mins.

ingredientes especiales

special ingredients

Harinas

Harina de garbanzos - frituras como bhajis y faláfel, salsas como bechamel, hamburguesas
Harina de arroz - frituras como tinas y sushi frito, hamburguesas, salsas
Harina de sarraceno (alforfón) - blinis, crêpes y pasteles
Harina de maíz - frituras como bolitas de maíz

Flours

Gram flour - fritters such as bhajis and falafels, sauces like bechamel, binding for mixes like hamburgers
Rice flour - fritters such as tinas and sushi frito, hamburgers, sauces
Buckwheat flour - blinis, crêpes and cakes
Maize flour - fritters such as corn fritters

Azúcares y sales

Jarabes y concentrados de fruta, arce, agave, manzana, remolacha, arroz
Tamari - parecido a la salsa de soja, sin gluten (siempre verificar etiqueta)
Marmite - extracto de levadura

Sugars and salts

Syrups and fruit concentrates - maple, agave, apple, beetroot, rice
Tamari - similar to soya sauce without gluten (but not always-check the label)
Marmite - yeast extract

Grasas

Aceite de oliva - platos mediterráneos y latinos
Aceite de girasol - platos orientales y asiáticos
Crema de coco - platos asiáticos
Margarina vegetal
Tahin - platos salados y pasteles

Fats

Olive oil - Mediterranean and Latin dishes
Sunflower oil - Asian and Oriental dishes
Creamed coconut - Asian and West Indian dishes
Vegetable margarine
Tahini - both savoury and sweet dishes

Leche

Soja
Arroz
Coco
y siempre existe la opción de sustituir con agua o zumo

Milk

Soya
Rice
Coconut
and there is always the option to substitute water or fruit juice

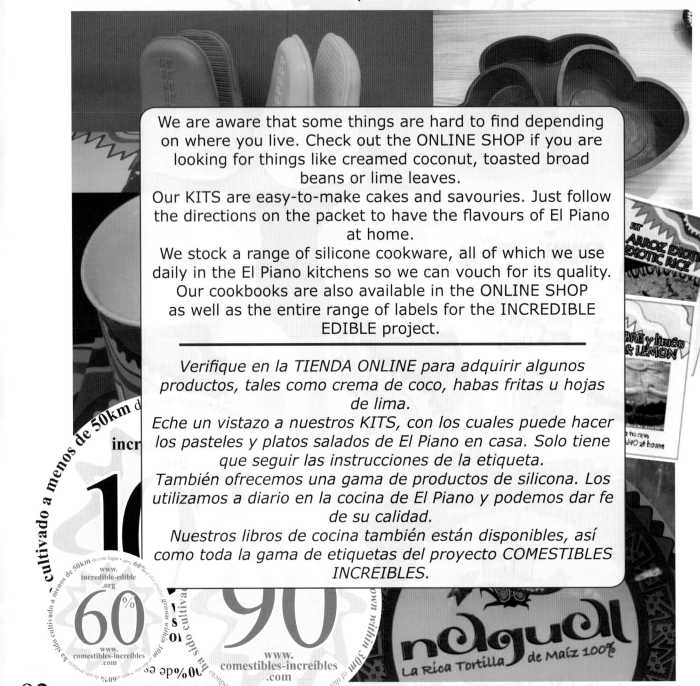

We are aware that some things are hard to find depending on where you live. Check out the ONLINE SHOP if you are looking for things like creamed coconut, toasted broad beans or lime leaves.

Our KITS are easy-to-make cakes and savouries. Just follow the directions on the packet to have the flavours of El Piano at home.

We stock a range of silicone cookware, all of which we use daily in the El Piano kitchens so we can vouch for its quality.

Our cookbooks are also available in the ONLINE SHOP as well as the entire range of labels for the INCREDIBLE EDIBLE project.

Verifique en la TIENDA ONLINE para adquirir algunos productos, tales como crema de coco, habas fritas u hojas de lima.

Eche un vistazo a nuestros KITS, con los cuales puede hacer los pasteles y platos salados de El Piano en casa. Solo tiene que seguir las instrucciones de la etiqueta.

También ofrecemos una gama de productos de silicona. Los utilizamos a diario en la cocina de El Piano y podemos dar fe de su calidad.

Nuestros libros de cocina también están disponibles, así como toda la gama de etiquetas del proyecto COMESTIBLES INCREIBLES.

coming soon   próximamente

Pam Warhurst, CBE was appointed as Chair of the Forestry Commission in 2009. Since then she has visited El Piano on a number of occasions and helped us formulate our policies for choosing suppliers and how to use our buildings to develop urban crops.

In 2012, working closely with Sacri López and Inocencio Ortega Naranjo of La Huerta Santa María, for the first time we brought organic AND local crops into daily use in EL PIANO GRANADA and EL PIANO MALAGA.

Inspired by Pam Warhurst and her work in Incredible Edible, in 2010 we began a York based initiative to unite EL PIANO YORK with other restaurants to start vertical growing of edible crops combined with ornamental plants. Phase 1 was planting edible crops in window boxes.

This initiative has been slow to develop but we hope in 2013 we will see the development of Phase 2, some smaller vertical growing in the EL PIANO YORK back yard, and Phase 3, a fully fledged green wall in 2014.

The York project has the support of the local authority, the Civic Trust, Askham Bryan Agricultural College, local schools as well as local growers. Watch this space...

En 2009 Pam Warhurst, CBE, fue nombrada la Presidenta de la Comisión de Silvicultura del Reino Unido. Desde entonces ha visitado El Piano algunas veces. Nos ha ayudado a crear nuestra política de proveedores de la zona y nos ha dado muchas ideas sobre el uso de nuestros edificios para progresar el cultivo urbano.

En 2012, al trabajar juntos con Sacri López e Inocencio Ortega Naranjo de La Huerta Santa María, por primera vez pudimos presentar en EL PIANO GRANADA y en EL PIANO MALAGA una cosecha diaria ecológica Y de la zona.

En EL PIANO YORK en 2010 empezamos otra iniciativa inspirada en el trabajo de Pam Warhurst y su proyecto Incredible Edible: la unión con otros restaurantes para desarrollar paredes verdes verticales en nuestros edificios con una combinación de plantas comestibles y ornamentales. Fase 1 fue plantas comestibles en macetas.

El proyecto ha sido lento pero esperamos que en 2013 se verá Fase 2, unas paredes verdes chicas en la terraza detrás de EL PIANO YORK, y en 2014 la última fase, una pared verde grande de plantas comestibles en la fachada.

El proyecto en York tiene el apoyo del ayuntamiento, el Civic Trust, la universidad de agricultura, colegios y los agricultores de la zona. A ver....

la visión the vision

At El Piano we try to create a seamless union between work and sustainability, through a focus on food, achieved through an independent, profitable, fun and transferable business model whose core principles are founded on the sustainability of the planet and the sustainability of one's private life.

En El Piano intentamos crear una unión invisible entre el trabajo y la sostenibilidad, integrando la sostenibilidad del planeta con la vida privada, a través de un modelo de negocio independiente, rentable, divertido y transferible.

Lo intentamos lograr de cinco maneras principales:

We work toward achieving this in five principle ways:

Vendiendo comida sin gluten y vegana a un precio razonable, pero con un alto rendimiento

Selling gluten free and vegan foods that are reasonably priced yet highly profitable

Asegurando a nuestros empleados unas condiciones flexibles para facilitar la vida familiar

Ensuring flexible working conditions to accommodate family life

Apoyando a trabajadores que desean desarrollar su propio El Piano

Supporting staff wishing to develop their own El Piano

Ahorrando energía mediante el uso de productos biodegradables, materiales reciclados, fuentes de calor multifuncionales, compartiendo vehículos, etc

Conserving energy through use of biodegradable and recycled materials, multi-functional heat sources, shared vehicles and so forth

Utilizando productos locales y ecológicos siempre que sea posible, y cultivando nuestros propios ingredientes

Using local and organic produce wherever possible, as well as growing our own

Si quiere saber más sobre quienes somos y lo que hacemos, visite la página web
www.el-piano.com
o contáctenos
info@el-piano.com

If you would like to know more about who we are and what we do, have a look at
www.el-piano.com
or contact us
info@el-piano.com

94

more books from
SQUAW PIES

más libros de
SQUAW PIES

HAND to MOUTH
2002
English
96 pages
full colour

HAND to MOUTH
mano a boca
2002
inglés
96 páginas
a todo color

HAND in HAND
2003
English
96 pages
full colour

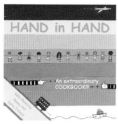

HAND in HAND
mano en mano
2003
inglés
96 páginas
a todo color

HANDING it ON
2009
English
96 pages
full colour

MANO a MANO
2009
español
96 páginas
a todo color

DOSSIER:

libros pequeños de 34 páginas a todo color, con recetas e info de productos de la zona trucos y consejos para preparar, comer y cultivar comida

DOSSIER:

little books of 34 full colour pages with recipes & info about local food tricks and tips for cooking, eating and growing food

y no sólo comida y cocina de SQUAW PIES...también hay...

and not just food and cooking from SQUAW PIES...there are also...

*...dos novelas de suspense de Anne Sikking...Basado en York, **FESTIVAL OF ANGELS** (solo en inglés). Basado en Granada, **CANCIÓN de GRANADA**... disponible en la tienda online y en versión digital en AMAZON en 2013*

...two thrillers from Anne Sikking... based in York, **FESTIVAL of ANGELS** (English only) and based in Granada, **SONG of GRANADA** ...available in the online shop as well as digitally through AMAZON from 2013

95

afterword

Roanne Mahony has been a lifelong inspiration. Sakina Begum and Shagufta Anwar were my Asian mentors. Miranda Castro and her father Roland took me to tastes I had never known. Kundia, bent, weathered and unspeakably poor, taught me everything I know about coconut.

I was lucky in aunts. Joy Turowski cooked simple perfectly seasoned food. Florine Sikking was a fabulous haute cusine cook. Marvel Kirby gave me her copy of The Joy of Cooking and periodically bought me wildly expensive gadgets. Peggy Thornton allowed me from infancy to stand on chairs to 'help'.

From these people and others I learned no matter how experienced the cook, how complex the recipe, how rare the ingredients, one thing is true. Cooking well is more than a skill or an art, it is a gift. It resides in love of food and in love of service alongside an instinct about flavour and colour.

This is my last cookbook. The next ones will be from the next generation of EL PIANO cooks. I wish for them that they love their work as much as I have and meet as many generous people.

epílogo

Roanne Mahony me ha inspirado mucho. Sakina Begum y Shagufta Anwar fueron mis mentoras de la cocina de Asia. Miranda Castro y su padre Roland me presentaron sabores totalmente desconocidos para mí. De Kundia, retorcido de dolor, insoportablemente pobre, aprendí todo lo que sé sobre el coco.

He tenido suerte con mis tías. Joy Turowski cocinaba comidas sencillas y perfectamente condimentadas. Florine Sikking fue una cocinera fabulosa de alta cocina. Marvel Kirby me dio su copia de The Joy of Cooking y de vez en cuando me compraba utensilios carísimos. Peggy Thornton me permitió desde la infancia subirme a una silla para 'ayudarla'.

De ellos y de otros aprendí que da igual la experiencia del cociner@, da igual si la receta es compleja o los ingredientes especiales, hay algo más fundamental. Cocinar bien es más que una habilidad, más que una forma de arte, es un don. Viene del amor de comer y de atender a los demás, junto a un instinto por sabores y colores.

Éste es mi último libro de cocina. Los siguientes serán de la generación nueva de cociner@s de EL PIANO. Espero que les encante su trabajo tanto como me ha encantado a mí y que encuentren por la vida gente tan generosa.

Magdalena Chávez - 2012